HOW DOES GOD ACT IN THE WORLD?

The Didsbury Lectures
Series Preface

The Didsbury Lectures, delivered annually at Nazarene Theological College, Manchester, are now a well-established feature on the theological calendar in Britain. The lectures are planned primarily for the academic and church community in Manchester but through their publication have reached a global readership.

The name "Didsbury Lectures" was chosen for its double significance. Didsbury is the location of Nazarene Theological College, but it was also the location of Didsbury College (sometimes known as Didsbury Wesleyan College), established in 1842 for training Wesleyan Methodist ministers.

The Didsbury Lectures were inaugurated in 1979 by Professor F. F. Bruce. He was followed annually by highly regarded scholars who established the series' standard. All have been notable for making high calibre scholarship accessible to interested and informed listeners.

The lectures give a platform for leading thinkers within the historic Christian faith to address topics of current relevance. While each lecturer is given freedom in choice of topic, the series is intended to address topics that traditionally would fall into the category of "Divinity." Beyond that, the college does not set parameters. Didsbury lecturers, in turn, have relished the privilege of engaging in the dialogue between church and academy.

Most Didsbury lecturers have been well-known scholars in the United Kingdom. From the start, the college envisaged the series as a means by which it could contribute to theological discourse between the church and the academic community more widely in Britain and abroad. The publication is an important part of fulfilling that goal. It remains the hope and prayer of the College that each volume will have a lasting and positive impact on the life of the church, and in the service of the gospel of Christ.

1979	Professor F. F. Bruce†	*Men and Movements in the Primitive Church*
1980	The Revd Professor I. Howard Marshall†	*Last Supper and Lord's Supper*
1981	The Revd Professor James Atkinson†	*Martin Luther: Prophet to the Church Catholic*
1982	The Very Revd Professor T. F. Torrance†	*The Mediation of Christ*
1983	The Revd Professor C. K. Barrett†	*Church, Ministry and Sacraments in the New Testament*
1984	The Revd Dr A. R. G. Deasley	*The Shape of Qumran Theology*
1985	Dr Donald P. Guthrie†	*The Relevance of John's Apocalypse*
1986	Professor A. F. Walls	*The Nineteenth-Century Missionary Movement***
1987	The Revd Dr A. Skevington Wood†	*Reason and Revelation*
1988	The Revd Professor Morna D. Hooker	*Not Ashamed of the Gospel: New Testament Interpretations of the Death of Christ*
1989	The Revd Professor Ronald E. Clements†	*Wisdom in Theology*
1990	The Revd Professor Colin E. Gunton†	*Christ and Creation*
1991	The Revd Professor J. D. G. Dunn†	*Christian Liberty: A New Testament Perspective*

1992	The Revd Dr P. M. Bassett†	*The Spanish Inquisition***
1993	Professor David J. A. Clines†	*The Bible in the Modern World*
1994	The Revd Professor James B. Torrance†	*Worship, Community, and the Triune God of Grace*
1995	The Revd Dr R. T. France†	*Women in the Church's Ministry*
1996	Professor Richard Bauckham	*God Crucified: Monotheism and Christology in the New Testament*
1997	Professor H. G. M. Williamson	*Variations on a Theme: King, Messiah and Servant in the Book of Isaiah*
1998	Professor David Bebbington	*Holiness in Nineteenth Century England*
1999	Professor L. W. Hurtado†	*At the Origins of Christian Worship*
2000	Professor Clark Pinnock†	*The Most Moved Mover: A Theology of God's Openness*
2001	Professor Robert P. Gordon	*Holy Land, Holy City: Sacred Geography and the Interpretation of the Bible*
2002	The Revd Dr Herbert McGonigle†	*John Wesley***
2003	Professor David F. Wright†	*What Has Infant Baptism Done to Baptism? An Enquiry at the End of Christendom*
2004	The Very Revd Dr Stephen S. Smalley†	*Hope for Ever: The Christian View of Life and Death*
2005	The Rt Revd Professor N. T. Wright	*Surprised by Hope***
2006	Professor Alan P. F. Sell†	*Nonconformist Theology in the Twentieth Century*
2007	Dr Elaine Storkey	*Sin and Social Relations***
2008	Dr Kent E. Brower	*Living as God's Holy People: Holiness and Community in Paul*
2009	Professor Alan Torrance	*Religion, Naturalism, and the Triune God: Confronting Scylla and Charybdis***
2010	Professor George Brooke	*The Dead Sea Scrolls and Christians Today***
2011	Professor Nigel Biggar	*Between Kin and Cosmopolis: An Ethic of the Nation*
2012	Dr Thomas A. Noble	*Holy Trinity: Holy People: The Theology of Christian Perfecting*
2013	Professor Gordon Wenham	*Rethinking Genesis 1–11*
2014	Professor Frances Young	*Construing the Cross: Type, Sign, Symbol, Word, Action*
2015	Professor Elaine Graham	*Apologetics without Apology*
2016	Professor Michael J. Gorman	*Missional Theosis in the Gospel of John*
2017	Professor Philip Alexander & Professor Loveday Alexander	*Priesthood and Sacrifice in the Epistle to the Hebrews***
2018	Professor Markus Bockmuehl	*The Four Evangelists on the Presence and Absence of Jesus***
2019	Professor Michael Lodahl	*Matthew Matters: The Yoke of Wisdom and the Church of Tomorrow*
2020	Professor John Swinton	*Deliver Us from Evil: A Call for Christians to Take Evil Seriously*
2021	Professor John Barclay	*Beyond Charity: Rethinking Gift and Community with Paul***
2022	Professor David Wilkinson	*How Does God Act in the World? Science, Miracle, and Mission*
2023	Professor Amos Yong	*Jesus in Cartographic Perspective***
2024	Professor John Behr	*In Accordance with the Scriptures*
2025	Dr Stephen Barton	

*** Not published in the series*

How Does God Act in the World?

Science, Miracle, and Mission

THE DIDSBURY LECTURES

DAVID WILKINSON

CASCADE *Books* • Eugene, Oregon

HOW DOES GOD ACT IN THE WORLD?
Science, Miracle, and Mission

The Didsbury Lectures Series

Copyright © 2025 David Wilkinson. All rights reserved. Except for brief quotations in critical publications or reviews, no part of this book may be reproduced in any manner without prior written permission from the publisher. Write: Permissions, Wipf and Stock Publishers, 199 W. 8th Ave., Suite 3, Eugene, OR 97401.

Cascade Books
An Imprint of Wipf and Stock Publishers
199 W. 8th Ave., Suite 3
Eugene, OR 97401

www.wipfandstock.com

PAPERBACK ISBN: 979-8-3852-0881-4
HARDCOVER ISBN: 979-8-3852-0882-1
EBOOK ISBN: 979-8-3852-0883-8

Cataloguing-in-Publication data:

Names: Wilkinson, David [author].

Title: How does God act in the world? : science, miracle, and mission / by David Wilkinson.

Description: Eugene, OR: Cascade Books, 2025 | Series: The Didsbury Lectures Series | Includes bibliographical references and index.

Identifiers: ISBN 979-8-3852-0881-4 (paperback) | ISBN 979-8-3852-0882-1 (hardcover) | ISBN 979-8-3852-0883-8 (ebook)

Subjects: LCSH: Religion and science. | Miracles. | Providence and government of God—Christianity. | Bible and science. | Causation.

Classification: BT135 W55 2025 (paperback) | BT135 (ebook)

05/23/25

For Leah Grace
As she grows up,
may she know that the God who loves her is at work in the world.

Contents

Acknowledgments xi

1. From the Clockwork of Newton to the Clouds of Weather Forecasting:
   Scientific Certainty and Uncertainty 1

2. A Science-Shaped God?
   Models of How God Acts in the World 19

3. The Messiness of Miracle:
   Exploring Scripture and Experience 51

4. Witnessing to a God Who Acts:
   Implications for Mission and Ministry in the Contemporary Church 77

Bibliography 107

General Index 129

Scripture Index 139

Acknowledgments

THESE DIDSBURY LECTURES WERE delivered at Nazarene Theological College in October 2022 with an additional seminar at the Department of Religions and Theology at Manchester University.

I am grateful to the Principal, Revd. Dr. Deidre Brower Latz, and staff of Nazarene Theological College for their hospitality and invitation to take part in this lecture series. I am also grateful for the questions, comments, and objections raised during the extended question and answer times. This has allowed me to reflect on, extend, and I hope to deepen the original material and revise it for this book. The range of different denominational and theological backgrounds represented in an audience of church leaders, lay Christians and academic theologians was invaluable in a subject area which itself spans so many disciplines and pastorally sensitive experiences. I am conscious however that many of the questions will remain unanswered.

Looking at the list of previous lecturers is both humbling and frightening! Many are my theological heroes and have shaped my own thinking not only in theology but also in the practice of mission and ministry. In particular, C. K. Barrett and J. D. G. Dunn, as both friends and mentors, gave me a deep respect for the complexity of the Scriptures but at the same time a sense that in its pages was a God who acts in grace. Again, I am grateful to them. But I am even more grateful for those outside the context of academic theology who have talked with me and pushed me to think more about these issues. In particular, for the past years, it has been a privilege to be part of Jesmond Methodist Church, where a belief in a God who acts has earthed me every week.

Finally, I am grateful to my wife, Alison, who lives, teaches, and preaches the death and resurrection of Jesus. From her I have learned the most.

David Wilkinson
September 14, 2024

1

From the Clockwork of Newton to the Clouds of Weather Forecasting

Scientific Certainty and Uncertainty

1.1 Introduction: Overview of Lectures

MY FIRST TERM AT University as a physics student was extraordinary. I had just started taking my Christian discipleship seriously, having had a conversion experience the previous summer. And then the first two courses in physics were relativity and quantum mechanics. This was a long way from some of the tedium of rolling wooden trolleys down benches in school science. This was a brand new world for me, both in terms of what Christian faith meant in understanding the world around but also in the mind-blowing concepts of time dilation, warped space-time, and the uncertainty of the quantum world.

In 2022 the Nobel Prize in Physics was given to Alain Aspect, John Clauser, and Anton Zeilinger for experimental work on quantum entanglement.[1] This award may have been submerged by other stories of the war in Ukraine and certain tangled political manoeuvres, but its importance should not be underestimated.

---

1. Amos, "Physics Nobel Rewards 'Spooky Science.'" See also Aspect et al., "Experimental Realization," 91–94; Aspect, "Quantum Mechanics," 866–67.

How Does God Act in the World?

Work on quantum entanglement opens exciting practical possibilities for quantum computing and secure encryption of communications. Yet this physics symbolizes and embodies a century of insights into the physical world that are surprising, intriguing, and puzzling for scientists. I will suggest in these lectures that these insights are also important for theologians, whether they be theologians in the academy or in the everyday life of church leaders and disciples.

Quantum entanglement, characterized by Albert Einstein as "spooky action at a distance," as we shall see, is a reminder that common sense is not a good guide to the nature of reality. This has been taken seriously by physicists but less seriously by theologians and the general public. And here we encounter an extremely important three-way conversation, namely that between science, theology, and the public square. Here the public square could be a local church congregation or it could be a school, but it certainly includes a media culture that cannot be ignored in theological thinking about mission and ministry in a scientific age.

In these lectures, I will be exploring the dialogue of science and theology in the area of a central theological question: How does God act in the world? From the practice of prayer to apologetic questions around the Covid pandemic, from miracles to the end of the universe, and within the climate emergency from human agency to God's sovereignty, underlying all these diverse issues lies the core question about divine action. This question has run through Christian history and remains crucial today in energizing and sustaining discipleship and witness.

My argument is reasonably simple, although it will take a good few pages to make it! First, science can both be a hindrance and help to Christian theologians exploring the question of how God acts in the world. Second, scientists are not the only conversation partners and should not be the dominating one. The question of how God acts in the world has been constrained within Western culture, shaped by the science of the day, sometimes to the exclusion of allowing other voices, such as the biblical material, tough questions from the problem of evil, and the witness of religious experience having their own valid and important contributions to the conversation. Third, this discussion has been focused on the dominance of the Newtonian worldview, initially welcomed by Christians as evidence for the argument from design but ultimately leading to a view of a god who could do little in the everyday events of life. While science has moved to a much more subtle and supple view of the world, some theologians and popular culture are still stuck with a picture that the last century has made redundant.

So, in this first lecture I will spend some time describing quantum theory and the more recent understanding of chaotic systems to illustrate the paucity of the Newtonian view. In the second lecture I will survey some of the current models of providence on offer within Western theology. I will then move on in the third lecture to look more specifically at miracle and in the fourth to ask how such theological models operate in mission and ministry in a post-Covid world.

In this first lecture, therefore, we need to grapple with some science, which might not be an easy ride for those who struggled with school physics. But this is an important foundation to establish for the rest of the lectures.

In this task I employ an unlikely ally, the theologian Walter Wink, a member of the Jesus Seminar. Wink commented, "People with an attenuated sense of what is possible will bring that conviction to the Bible and diminish it by the poverty of their own experience."[2] On the road to quantum entanglement, we will see that science can enrich the poverty of our experience and expand our sense of what is possible.

1.2 From Aristotle to Newton: The Dominance of a Mechanistic Universe

When Galileo Galilei (1564–1642) pointed his newly invented telescope at the night sky in 1610 he illustrated that empirical science has a way of disrupting widely held philosophical and theological views based on the poverty of experience. The Aristotelian universe, baptized into Christian belief by Thomas Aquinas, was constructed on the belief that the sphere, to the human mind, was the most perfect shape, and this was the way the universe was. With the Earth at the center, the planets were carried in their motion across the night sky on perfect crystalline spheres. Only within the orbit of the Moon did objects move in straight lines. When the planetary orbits did not quite fit, Ptolemy had used spheres upon spheres, epicycles, to explain the anomalies.

As observation began to take more center stage, this commitment to self-evident axioms began to falter. Tycho Brahe (1546–1601) observed a comet moving in a straight line beyond the orbit of the Moon and also saw

2. Wink, "Write What You See," 6.

a supernova explosion, which we now know was a star coming to the end of its life.[3] Lights appearing in the sky apparently from nowhere did not fit well with Aristotle.

Galileo's *Starry Messenger* (1610) and *Letters on Sunspots* (1613) showed other features that undermined Aristotle. The surface of the Moon was not perfect, with craters and mountains, and the Sun had spots on its face. His observations of the moons of Jupiter and the phases of Venus providing not proof but support for the Copernican model of the solar system.[4]

Copernicus (1473–1543) of course had published his model some seventy years earlier but had been spared some of the opposition that would come to Galileo—partly because of his death shortly after the publication of his *On the Revolutions of the Celestial Spheres* (1543) but also because Lutheran pastor Andreas Osiander had suggested in his preface to the book that this was just a calculating device rather than a description of reality.[5]

Galileo's observations took this a step forward, indicating that the Copernican model was indeed a description of reality. The opposition from the Roman Catholic Church was focused not on a mythical "science disproves the Bible" debate but on the challenge first to Aristotle and second to the nature of doing science. Tommaso Caccini in a sermon in Florence 1614 summed this up in a clever word play on Acts 1:11, "You man of Galilee, why do you stand gazing up to the heavens."[6] This was a revolution in science, moving the emphasis from earthbound observations and a commitment to figuring out the universe through human logic to the importance of empirical science, which went beyond everyday experience.

Nevertheless, the importance of seeing the continuity between experience on Earth and experience of the heavens was illustrated later in the same century in a garden in Woolsthorpe. The plague of 1665 had driven Isaac Newton (1642–1727) home from being a student at Cambridge. In this lockdown, apparently hit on the head by an apple (so the story goes), he was stimulated to develop a whole array of new streams of understanding the natural world. This included his laws of motion, binomial theorem, differential and integral calculus, the composite nature of white light, and his universal law of gravitation:

---

3. Christianson, *Tycho Brahe and the Measure of the Heavens*.
4. Heilbron, *Galileo*; Sharratt, *Galileo*.
5. Gingerich, *Book Nobody Read*; "Copernicus and Tycho," 86–101.
6. Finocchiaro, *Galileo Affair*, 330.

From the Clockwork of Newton to the Clouds

$$f = \frac{Gm_1 m_2}{r^2}$$

Here the force between two bodies can be expressed by the multiplication of their individual masses (m) divided by the square of the distance between them (r) and multiplied by the value of a constant (G).

The culmination of this work was published in *Principia* in 1687. Here was the application of simple and elegant mathematics not just to the Earth but beyond. Applying it to the motion of planets around the Sun, it was able to predict where the planets were in the past and where they would be in the future. This was a universe that was both predictable and picturable. Victorian dining rooms would have in pride of place an orrery, a mechanical wind-up model showing the planets orbiting the Sun. The first orrery was produced at the beginning of the eighteenth century, and was presented to Charles Boyle, Fourth Earl of Orrery.

But this development was not without its unanswered questions. How did the gravitational force act? Some, such as the deist Anthony Collins (1676–1729), saw it as due to active principles associated with but not inherent in matter. William Whiston (1667–1752) saw it as the direct expression of God's continual activity. Newton, as a theist, believed in a God who was the origin of the planetary orbits, as initial conditions were simply assumed by his theory. But even then, he still had a problem. Would the universe slowly collapse due to the same law of gravity? The stability of the fixed stars needed, in Newton's mind, the occasional intervention of God, pushing them back into place. As John Brooke has written, "God had taken every precaution to minimise the destabilising forces and yet had willed a world in which His intervention would also be required."[7]

Perhaps even more challenging was whether the universe would run down. Here Newton's understanding was developed by Leibniz (1646–1716) and Laplace (1749–1827). They would show that Newton did not need an interventionist God to guarantee the stability of the solar system, with Leibniz writing concerning Nature, "I maintain it to be a watch, that goes without wanting to be mended by him."[8] In fact, a story is told of Laplace presenting Napoleon with his work to which Napoleon replies, "I gather there is no mention of God in this work." Laplace replies "Sir, I have no

---

7. Brooke, *Science and Religion*, 147.
8. Leibniz, *Philosophical Papers and Letters*, 679.

need of this hypothesis."[9] The actual exchange and meaning of the words used is much debated, but the story gives the sense that Newton's interventionist God was to be rejected in favor of the perfect watchmaker whose watches did not need constant attention.

It follows that the idea of a perfect watchmaker and the universe as a perfect clock gave considerable energy to the design argument for the existence of God. Robert Boyle (1627–1691) was one of many leading scientists of the day who saw the universe as a great clock and argued for design in nature in sermons, lectures, and publications, such as the Boyle Lectures and The Bridgewater Treatises. This would find its summit in William Paley's (1743–1805) *Natural Theology* and his classic watchmaker analogy for a God of design.[10]

Yet just as the universe as a picturable and predictable clock was taking away a God of imperfect design and offering an attempted proof of a perfect designer's existence, it was simultaneously distancing God from any involvement in the universe. This was by far its most serious theological legacy, which, as we shall see, would have consequences for biblical interpretation, philosophical and systematic theology, and, even more importantly, mission and ministry.

Where was God in all of this? One option was deism.[11] Here God was the one who started the whole universe off but then had no more to do with it. At the other end of the spectrum, pantheism saw everything in the universe as part of an all-encompassing, immanent God. Both saw little space for God to do anything particular in the perfect clock that the Newtonian system was describing.[12]

Now it is important to note, as Peter Harrison has pointed out, that while deism or pantheism may be the legacy of the Newton's mechanistic universe, the scientists of the day did not rule out God working by miracles.[13] Newton and Boyle, for example, seemed to have an inconsistent belief in both a mechanical universe governed by scientific laws alongside the belief in an omnipotent God who intervened by breaking those laws. Indeed, for Boyle, miracles could be seen as evidence for establishing the

---

9. De Morgan, *Budget of Paradoxes*, 249.
10. Dolnick, *Clockwork Universe*.
11. Wigelsworth, *Deism in Enlightenment England*.
12. Cooper, *Panentheism*.
13. Harrison, "Newtonian Science," 531–53.

truth of Christianity.[14] However, Harrison helpfully argues that such apparent inconsistency can be avoided once we understand that, for Newton and others, the definition of a miracle did not involve a violation of the laws of nature. We shall return to miracle in lecture 3, but it worth pausing here. Harrison notes that for Augustine the core of miracle was the unusualness of its occurrence in God's actions. Both the mundane and the unusual were the acting of God. This was reformulated by Samuel Clarke and Newton, avoiding language of "breaching the laws of nature" and seeing many miracles as *unusual coincidences in causes*. This was dependent on seeing the laws of nature not as absolute entities in themselves but rather created and sustained by the continuous action of God.

Yet to many, a mechanistic universe did not have this subtlety. A perfect designer would not poke fingers into the perfect clock. Such a picture of God did help with responses to the problem of evil, for it claimed that God could not intervene in the world even if God wanted to. The consequence of the mechanical picture of the universe was that it encouraged a deistic view of God and gave a philosophical framework for seeing biblical miracles as stories created by the early church to express theological truth rather than a record of God's unusual activity in history.

1.3 The Demolition of the Mechanistic Universe: Twentieth-Century Physics

It had to wait until the twentieth century before it became clear that the world on the smallest of scales, such as protons and electrons, was *not* picturable or predictable in the way it had been portrayed by the clockwork universe of Newton. Even on the scale of everyday macro systems, such as the weather, the simple systems that had been described by Newton did not account for the unpredictability of the world.

Contrary to the widespread objection, championed by new atheism and some sections of the media, that theology and science are in conflict, the actual relationship between theology and the sciences is far more fruitful and intriguing as a result of these insights. As Pannenberg rightly commented:

> Curiously enough this objection is seldom raised by scientists nowadays, and least of all physicists; it is most often heard on the

---

14. Westfall, *Science and Religion*, 89, 200; Burns, *Great Debate on Miracles*, 12.

lips of theologians, or even historians. In these quarters a dogmatic view of the natural sciences is evidently still widespread which is no longer held by the sciences themselves.[15]

In particular, in the words of John Polkinghorne, these developments in twentieth-century science developed a view of the universe as "subtle" and "supple,"[16] in great contrast to the rigidity and completeness of the clockwork mechanism of Newtonian physics. It is to quantum theory and to chaos that we now turn.

1.3.1 Quantum Theory: Unpicturable and Unpredictable

At the beginning of the twentieth century, the foundations of the Newtonian worldview were secure and had enabled physics to understand and manipulate the world. For example, Maxwell's formulation of the equations of electromagnetism was a strong explanatory tool allowing the development of new technologies. The perceived universality of the laws of Newton and Maxwell engendered an optimism that science was all-conquering.

However, there were one or two minor questions that were stubborn in resisting solution. The orbit of Mercury did not quite fit, and the spectrum of radiation given off by a heated body was not what was expected. It needed a revolution in physics to deal with these questions. Einstein's relativity showed that Newton's understanding of gravity and motion was a very limited view of reality, and quantum theory took us to an understanding of the world at an atomic level that was completely different from our everyday experience.[17]

As I write this lecture, I am utilizing the practical outworking of quantum theory. Modern semi-conductors in my laptop and my phone are designed in the light of the quantum nature of matter. Without the insights of quantum theory, there would be no lasers, nuclear power, or the electron microscope. Its technology shapes our world, and yet, since its formulation in the early part of the twentieth century, it is difficult to understand in terms of everyday experience. Indeed, it has generated a number of questions that remain puzzling to physicists and philosophers alike.[18]

15. Pannenberg, *Apostles' Creed*, 110.
16. Polkinghorne, *Quantum World*.
17. Agar, *Science in the Twentieth Century*.
18. George, *Quantum World*; Maudlin, *Philosophy of Physics*; Zwiebach, *Mastering Quantum Mechanics*.

From the Clockwork of Newton to the Clouds

While the world of Newton is picturable and predictable, the quantum world is unpicturable and unpredictable, with events being uncaused. For example, the Uncertainty Principle of Werner Heisenberg says that you cannot know precisely both the position and the momentum (that is, its velocity multiplied by its mass) of a particle. You can know *where it is* or *how it is travelling* but *not both*.

Let's try and illustrate this in a different way. In his theory of electromagnetism, Maxwell had described light as a propagating wave of electric and magnetic fields. The wave properties of light had been known since 1801 in the work of Thomas Young.[19] Passing a light through a slit in a barrier led to a characteristic diffraction pattern, which was formed on the screen behind. Opening up a second slit close to the first slit led to a different pattern of light and dark fringes on the same screen. This was characteristic of wave motion. But then a couple of ground-breaking discoveries suggested that in fact light was particle-like, as photons or quanta of energy. This was the only explanation of Max Planck's work on electromagnetic radiation from heated bodies (1900) and Albert Einstein's work on the emission of electrons when a metal surface was bathed in ultra-violet radiation (1905).[20] Was light a wave or a particle? It certainly demonstrated both wave and particle characteristics.

If light demonstrated particle characteristics, might particles such as electrons demonstrate wave characteristics? In 1927 experiments showed that this was indeed the case.[21] So what would happen if you passed electrons through the double slit experiment described above? A beam of electrons was directed at a screen. With a barrier with two open slits between the source and the screen, the pattern of fringes characteristic of wave motion appeared. Let's call this Pattern A. With one of the slits covered, the electrons form a different pattern on the screen the same as light. Let's call this Pattern B.

With a beam of electrons, we can send just one electron at a time through the double slit experiment and see where it falls on the screen. But does it fall on Pattern A (two slits open) or Pattern B (one slit open)? If it reaches the screen, it must have gone through one of the slits in the barrier. Therefore, when it reaches the screen, it should fall on the Pattern B, which is related to one slit. However, as you do the experiment, the electrons going

---

19. Young, "Bakerian Lecture," 1–16.
20. Planck, "Ueber das Gesetz," 553; Einstein, "On a Heuristic Viewpoint," 132–48.
21. Davisson and Germer, "Scattering of Electrons," 558; Thomson and Reid, "Diffraction of Cathode Rays," 890.

through individually fall on Pattern A, which is characteristic of two slits. The bizarre but inescapable conclusion of this is that the electron passes through both slits. How can that be? The quantum explanation is not to talk of where the electron *actually is* but to talk in terms of *probability*. You cannot say that the electron passed through one slit as opposed to the other, you can only calculate its probability of passing through one slit and its probability of passing through the other. Such a situation is impossible to picture in everyday terms and to talk of causes becomes irrelevant.[22]

If there is difficulty describing the quantum micro-world in terms of our experience of the everyday macro-world, there is a further problem in trying to understand how the quantum world and the everyday world are physically related. How does the uncertain quantum world give certain answers when interrogated by our everyday world? How does a world of uncertainty and probability allow me to put my laptop on a table and type, for both the laptop and the table are composed of protons, neutrons, and electrons. A century on from the development of quantum theory, this remains a question without a universally accepted answer. There have been a number of suggestions to what is known as the measurement problem. The Copenhagen interpretation, favored by Werner Heisenberg, Niels Bohr, and most physicists, suggests that the intervention of macro-world measuring instruments "collapses" the probability of the quantum world into a definite measurement.[23] Yet the very measuring instruments are themselves composed of atoms that have quantum behavior. To solve this problem, Neumann, Wigner, and Wheeler suggested that it is the intervention of *a conscious observer* that leads to a measurement.[24] This does run the same problem of the brain being composed of atoms, but it might be argued that the complex relationship between mind and brain could provide a solution. A completely different solution to the problem was proposed by Hugh Everett III in his many-worlds interpretation, where in every act of measurement *each possibility available is realized*, and at that point the universe splits into separate universes corresponding to the realized possibilities.[25]

---

22. Ananthaswamy, *Through Two Doors at Once*.

23. Heisenberg, *Physics and Philosophy*, 28; Folse and Faye, *Niels Bohr*.

24. Neumann, *Mathematical Foundations of Quantum Mechanics*; Wigner and Margenau, "Remarks on the Mind Body Question," 1169–70; Wheeler and Zurek, *Quantum Theory and Measurement*.

25. Barrett and Byrne, *Everett Interpretation of Quantum Mechanics*.

The second puzzling question of quantum theory is: What does quantum theory tell us about the nature of reality? What is the relationship between epistemology and ontology? The majority of physicists take the view that uncertainty is in the nature of reality rather than the view that it is just a limit on our knowledge. A minority, including de Broglie and Bohm, believe that there must be a deeper theory that explains the apparent uncertainty of quantum theory.[26]

Even with these unanswered questions the implications for our view of reality and the arena of speculation for some contemporary theologians are profound.[27] To this we will return in a moment. However, there have been some who have said that uncertainty at the quantum level has little to do with our experience as agents in the everyday world and God's agency in human experience. To this, the latter part of the twentieth century placed alongside quantum theory another area of profound uncertainty which was very much part of everyday human experience.

1.3.2 Chaos: Deterministic but Unpredictable

In 1961 Edward Lorenz, reliant on programmers Ellen Fetter and Margaret Hamilton, was using an early digital computer to run weather simulations. By inputting data such as temperature and pressure and using models of the atmosphere that had been well developed, they could simulate weather patterns to help in forecasting. Wanting to repeat a simulation but also wanting to save time, they started the simulation halfway through, entering by hand the data from a printout that corresponded to this time in the simulation. They were startled to see that the computer predicted weather completely different to the initial simulation. They saw that this had been due to the data on the printout being rounded off to a three-digit number rather than the six-digit number used by the computer. By inputting the rounded number, they had used a number fractionally different. The expectation was that the difference was so small that it should not have made any difference. However, what they had discovered was that even very small differences in initial conditions led to massive changes in future

---

26. Bohm, "Suggested Interpretation of the Quantum Theory I," 166–79; "Suggested Interpretation of the Quantum Theory II," 180–93; Holland, *Quantum Theory of Motion*.

27. See, for example, Ó Murchú, *Quantum Theology*; Polkinghorne, *Quantum Physics and Theology*; Russell, *Quantum Mechanics*; Simmons, *Entangled Trinity*.

predictions.[28] The system was still deterministic in that the laws were well-known and there was no random chance intruding into the process. Yet it was so sensitive to initial conditions that it was unpredictable. In chaotic systems the smallest fluctuations get amplified. Lorenz would speak of how even a seagull flapping its wings might eventually make a big difference to the weather. This evolved in 1972 to the image of a butterfly flapping its wings leading to a hurricane.[29]

Therefore, accurate weather predictions fail at some point in the future not because we do not understand how the atmosphere works but because its initial state can never be measured accurately enough. Lorenz had suggested a couple of weeks was as far as accurate predictions could reach, which is roughly the time that we now experience to be the case.[30]

This was a very different world to the Newtonian mechanistic universe, but it was also the world of the everyday, of macro systems such as the weather, fluid flow, heartbeat irregularities, and even road traffic.[31] Newton had described some systems where the laws were determined and thought that this meant that once you defined its state at one time then all future states were determined. However, a chaotic system is a deterministic system in the sense that you understand its laws, but that does not mean that its future can be predicted from its current state.[32]

It is important to stress at this time that the unpredictability comes from the small differences in specifying the initial conditions of the system, either due to our inability to measure them with sufficient exactness or the inability of computers to do the numerical computation without rounding errors. At that level one might think this is simply an epistemological uncertainty due to our limitations to do the measurements and calculations. However, the way the unpredictability grows in chaotic systems means that very quickly you need computers greater than the universe to do the calculations. Does that mean that the systems are unpredictable not just in practice but also in principle?

---

28. Lorenz, "Deterministic Non-Periodic Flow," 130–41.
29. Lorenz, "Does the Flap of a Butterfly's Wings."
30. Gleick, *Chaos*; Kellert, *In the Wake of Chaos*; Crutchfield et al., "Chaos" 38–49.
31. Weinberger, *Everyday Chaos*.
32. Werndl, "What Are the New Implications of Chaos," 195–220.

1.4 Theological Implications

We now turn to at least raise some of the theological issues that we will need to return to in subsequent chapters.

1.4.1 Limits of a Newtonian Worldview

The most profound issue is that quantum theory and chaos show the limits of the Newtonian worldview as a description of reality. Newton's clockwork universe gives us a very limited view of a very small part of the world. Some systems are deterministic in the predictable way that former generations of physicists imagined. But to generalize a view of reality based on these systems is misleading, both scientifically and theologically. As Karl Popper commented, the universe of the twentieth century contains both clocks and clouds.[33]

In 1986, three hundred years after Newton's *Principia Mathematica* was presented to the Royal Society, the International Union of Theoretical and Applied Mechanics made an extraordinary public apology:

> We collectively wish to apologize for having misled the general educated public by spreading ideas about the determinism of systems satisfying Newton's laws of motion that, after 1960, were proved to be incorrect.... Modern theories of dynamical systems have clearly demonstrated the unexpected fact that systems governed by the equations of Newtonian dynamics do not necessarily exhibit the "predictability" property.[34]

As we shall see, twentieth-century theology might consider making a similar apology for being wedded to an outdated view of science in the mechanistic universe. Here we also see the danger of what Polkinghorne called the tyranny of common sense. Common sense, based on our everyday experience of certain predictable systems, should not be extrapolated to understand the nature of the universe and then, indeed, the nature of God.

---

33. Popper, *Of Clouds and Clocks*.
34. Lighthill, "Recently Recognized Failure," 35.

1.4.2 Intelligibility as Key to Reality

If quantum theory breaks the tyranny of common sense, then does its inability to describe the world in everyday terms mean that nothing can really be known about reality? If both position and momentum cannot be simultaneously specified for an electron, can we say anything beyond the claim that all is mystery? Do we just accept that both science and theology play the apophatic card and get on with the few things we can understand?

This is unsatisfactory to the physicist who notes that not all the questions of quantum theory have easy and agreed solutions, but its mathematical formulation means that we can do important things with it in both understanding and working with physical reality. This role of mathematics as a language that helps to express and communicate the quantum world rather than everyday pictures and analogies should not be underestimated. Here there is an interesting link with the thinking of Roman Catholic philosopher, theologian, and economist Bernard Lonergan. Lonergan proposed a "generalized empirical method" (GEM) as a way of understanding our view of the world. This was similar to what others would call critical realism. In this, scientific models were not complete and final descriptions of reality. They involve the role of the human mind within community, interpreting observational data and constructing models. Yet unlike Kant they did describe, even in a limited and provisional way, a reality beyond our minds. Lonergan's thinking was represented in two major works, *Insight: A Study of Human Understanding* and *Method in Theology*. He suggested that intelligibility is the clue to reality. Thus, the business of empirical science is to study immanent intelligibility, stressing primarily correlations rather than causes.[35] This led him to an argument for the existence of God based on intelligibility rather than first causes—that is, "If the real is completely intelligible, God exists. But the real is completely intelligible. Therefore, God exists." The intelligibility we assume in the universe needs an intelligible ground.

While the argument for the existence of God may not be accepted by other philosophers, the stress on intelligibility is helpful in the context of quantum theory. A move away from arguments on first causes to coherent understandings of the world may lead to what Polkinghorne called a revised natural theology.

---

35. Crowe, "Bernard Lonergan's Thought," 58–89.

Lonergan also leads us to our next observation: the limits of reductionism. A holistic account of the relationship between observer and the observed questions any reductionist metaphysics.

1.4.3 The Subverting of Reductionism

Science proceeds by methodological reductionism. That is, a system is broken down into smaller parts in the attempt to understand the whole. But the mistake of philosophical reductionism is to believe that once you have understood each part of the system you therefore understand the whole. The mistake is beautifully satirized by a John Cleese sketch where, lampooning a scientist, he claims that there are individual genes that explain everything from why we believe in God to why we watch Nicholas Cage movies![36]

Yet quantum and chaotic systems are a reminder that this is far too simplistic. Because of the effect of small differences, such systems are never truly isolated. This had already been seen in the concept of emergence, where complexity means that a system can never be reduced to its parts. Complexity itself allows new phenomenon to emerge that cannot be explained by the behavior of its components. This idea was pursued by the biologist and theologian Arthur Peacocke.[37] It is important to be clear that any completeness or incompleteness of lower-level models does not imply the redundancy of higher-level descriptions.[38]

Yet there is one further aspect of quantum theory that is important for this, and here we return to "spooky action at a distance." Although awarded the Nobel prize a century ago for beginning the field of quantum theory, Albert Einstein had severe reservations about its philosophical interpretation famously summed up in his "God does not play dice with the universe." In 1935, Einstein, along with colleagues Boris Podolsky and Nathan Rosen, proposed a thought experiment, the EPR paradox, which they argued showed that quantum theory was not a complete description of reality.[39] They attempted to show that two quantum particles, such as photons, according to quantum theory, should retain the ability to influence each other even though extremely large distances separate them. This went against what we often take for granted, that an event in one part of

---

36. Cleese, "God Gene."
37. Peacocke, "Emergence, Mind, and Divine Action," 256–78.
38. Sharpe and Walgate, "Emergent Order," 411–33.
39. Einstein et al., "Can Quantum-Mechanical Description," 777–80.

the world cannot instantly affect other events far away, called by physicists "locality." Thus, for Einstein, quantum theory was suspect and incomplete.

In 1964 John Bell, in a theorem that bears his name, showed that locality could be tested and quantum theory predicted stronger statistical correlations in the outcomes of certain measurements separated by far distances.[40] Following this, in the early 1980s, it was Aspect and his colleagues who showed in real experiments that on this matter Einstein was wrong. They used calcium atoms excited to a particular high-energy state, from which the atoms decay by emitting two photons (one red, one blue). When those two photons are emitted in opposite directions, their polarizations are entangled in exactly the right way to test Bell's theorem. Particles even separated by vast distances are entangled, a property that John Polkinghorne characterized as "togetherness in separation."

This led to not only a "non-local" view of the world but also the field of quantum information science and quantum computing. The world is more surprising, stranger, and entangled than Newton would ever have imagined.

1.4.4 Locating God at Work?

For several faith communities, quantum theory has become a subject that resonates with their religious insights or has become a space in which to see God at work.

The "togetherness in separation" and uncertainty of the quantum world have led some popular writers, such as Capra and Zukav, to find parallels with Buddhism and certain streams of Hinduism.[41] These parallels have been rejected by others as superficial.[42] In fact, some see this quantum mysticism as pseudoscience or "quantum quackery," misrepresenting both the science and the religious tradition.[43]

The nature of a faith tradition such as Hinduism is complex with several different spiritual and theological understandings. It is therefore an easy tendency to find resonance with one strand and with one interpretation of quantum theory over which, as we have seen, there still is no general

---

40. Bell, "On the Einstein Podolsky Rosen Paradox," 195–200.
41. See, e.g., Capra, *Tao of Physics*; Zukav, *Dancing Wu Li Masters*.
42. Bussey, "Eastern Religions and Modern Physics," 113–27; Clifton and Regehr, "Capra on Mysticism and Modern Physics," 53.
43. Ascari, "From Spiritualism to Syncretism," 9–21.

agreement. In addition, while stressing, for example, the uncertainty and connectedness of quantum theory, the mathematical coherence and non-quantum aspects of the world can be downplayed. Such lessons are not only important for this critique of Capra and Zukav, they are important warnings for Christian theologians wanting to employ quantum theory.

Yet for a number of twentieth-century thinkers in the field of science and Christian theology, both quantum theory and chaos have been attractive as giving space to God acting in the world unconstrained by the predictability of deterministic systems.[44] Here the science is taken seriously and brought into conversation with mainstream theology.

In 1990 Sir John Eccles argued that the openness of quantum processes could explain human freewill.[45] The mechanistic universe had often been a problem for the proponents of true human freewill and agency. For if the science of body and brain could be fully understood, would that not imply that any freewill was illusory? Eccles felt that human freedom could find an unconstrained space in the uncertainty of the quantum world. As a Roman Catholic he explored science, faith, and the soul from within this perspective.

In a similar way, William Pollard, a physicist and Episcopal priest, saw quantum theory as the location of God's providence.[46] God finds space to work in a way that does not break laws and remains hidden. Many have followed in more thoughtful and creative ways, such as Robert Russell, who sees the possibility of God working at the quantum level, especially when in the early stages of the universe processes were all in the realm of the quantum world.[47] This is a fair point and a reminder that we cannot simply think about God's action only in a universe of which we have had direct experience.

Yet for Polkinghorne this was unconvincing, in large part because of one of the big unanswered questions of quantum theory—that is, how does the quantum world relate to the everyday world? It is difficult to see how God working at the uncertainty of the quantum level would affect the everyday level.

In contrast, Polkinghorne saw that chaos might allow God the freedom to act in a way that truly changed the everyday world.[48] This involved

---

44. Russell et al., *Chaos and Complexity*.

45. Eccles, "Unitary Hypothesis of Mind-Brain Interaction"; Eccles, *How the Self Controls Its Brain*.

46. Pollard, *Chance and Providence*.

47. Russell, "Quantum Physics."

48. Polkinghorne, *Science and Providence*.

an important step. Polkinghorne was a committed critical realist, seeing scientific theories as provisional and limited but also aiming to achieve verisimilitude; that is, they strive to reflect more clearly ontological reality. This meant that he made a strong link between epistemology and ontology. The practical unpredictability of chaotic systems therefore pointed to an ontological unpredictability or openness to the future. This openness could then be the location of both human freedom and God's freedom to act in a way that was hidden. As Stephen Hawking once quipped, "God does play dice, and sometimes he throws them where we can't see." Polkinghorne extends this freedom to the physical universe itself. It is therefore as God's freedom to act and human freedom to act interact with this inherent openness in physical process that questions of providence could be understood.

This then provides some of the questions for the next lecture. We have seen that Newton describes a very small part of reality and that the clockwork universe is not a good understanding. The universe is more supple and subtle, and for some this raises the question of whether the openness of the universe gives God freedom to act. That may be the science, but the science will need to be in dialogue with theological insights. The lesson of the mechanistic universe was that a perception of science dominated theology. We should not repeat the mistake with quantum theory and chaos.

2

A Science-Shaped God?

Models of How God Acts in the World

IN THE FIRST LECTURE of this series, I argued that the predictability of a clockwork model of the physical universe had been superseded by the unpredictability and the bizarre world of both chaos and quantum theory. Of course, such unpredictability and the difficultly of understanding reality has in recent years been at the heart of British politics!

On October 25, 2022, Rishi Sunak became the fifth prime minister since the Conservatives became the party of government, taking over from previous prime ministers, who had presided over bizarre European withdrawal deals, the response to a pandemic, and a budget statement that had led to panic in the markets and a crashing of the economy, which in turn would affect the cost of living most seriously for the poorest in society. The *Sun* newspaper on October 24, 2022, led with the headline, "THE FORCE IS WITH YOU: Tory MPs Turn to *Star Wars* Fan Rishi Sunak as 'New Hope' Without Single Vote Being Cast." The headline went with a Photoshopped picture of the new prime minister holding a light saber. The editor was certainly doing overtime with the *Star Wars* references!

Such a reference to *Star Wars* allows us a little diversion at the beginning of this lecture. The creator of *Star Wars*, George Lucas, used the concept of "The Force" to argue that there is something deeper to the universe than that which science can describe and technology can control. The small band of rebels triumph over the military might of the Empire and the technological power of the Death Star by trusting in this strange and mysterious reality interwoven with the nature of the universe.[1] Pop culture of course works not by giving answers or giving a new religion to believe in (despite what some of its fans sometimes think), but it uses stories to pose questions. As Lucas commented on the Force:

> I would hesitate to call the Force God. It's designed primarily to make young people think about mystery. Not to say, "Here's the answer." It's to say, "Think about this for a second. Is there a God? What does God look like? What does God sound like? What does God feel like? How do we relate to God?"[2]

However, there are other questions being asked within *Star Wars*. How much are the events of history random political decisions borne out of complete freedom of agency or how much are they being guided by mysterious forces beyond our understanding? The opening of the first movie of the *Star Wars* narrative arc, *The Phantom Menace,* was derided by some for locating the rise of an evil empire and emperor in a minor trade dispute on an insignificant outer planet. Two things may be going on here. The first is to ask whether evil can arise out of what may seem to be minor decisions but also to ask whether such things become part of a master plan of those who manipulate apparent freedom for their own purposes.

Indeed, the confirmation of Rishi Sunak raises deeper questions of democracy. What is human agency in all of this? Are we, as the electorate, just cogs in the wheel with no options to make a difference?

It may seem a long way from Rishi Sunak through *Star Wars* to the doctrine of providence. Yet providence is the attempt to understand God's agency in the universe in relation to our own agency in the universe. At its heart is the question of what is God like in God's power and compassion towards the universe? It is a central theological question of the nature of God in relation to creation, and it has deep implications for ministry in apologetics and pastoral care. For the scientist who works with the physical universe and sees science as a Christian vocation, the question of providence is sharpened in daily life.

For some, the appeal to mystery here can be very attractive. Yet I am not fully convinced. In one of his stand-up shows, *Fame*, the comedian

---

1. Wilkinson, *Power of the Force.*
2. Moyers and Lucas, "Cinema."

Ricky Gervais recounts pushing his school's Religious Studies teacher as to why there is suffering in the world if there is a loving God. The teacher's recourse to "It's a mystery" is interpreted by Gervais as someone who says, "Oh, look over there!" and then tries to run away when you turn to look. Now the problem of evil does not have simple answers, and any cursory knowledge of Christian theology will know this to be the case. I was once on a live question-and-answer session on BBC local radio and the interviewer said to me, "We have thirty seconds before the news. . . . Let me ask you how as a Christian you can understand war, famine, and injustice." In that context, I had to say, "I don't have an answer in twenty-five seconds, and, indeed, I don't have a full answer even if we had longer, but there are some things that can be said about the God who is revealed in Jesus." A doctrine of providence may not give easy models or answers, but that is not to say that it cannot give some insights into God's action and our action in the world.[3]

2.1 Evil and Openness: Providence in Contemporary Theology

In the twentieth century and through to the twenty-first century, questions of providence have been center stage in theological discourse, and there have been a number of distinct influences shaping that discourse.

2.1.1 The Rise of Biblical Theology

First, a re-emphasis on the Bible being a proclamation of divine action. This can be seen in Karl Barth's passion for a God who was encountered in revelation and on through to the biblical theology movement of the mid-twentieth century.[4] This movement saw the Bible as a theological resource, arguing for its unity and uniqueness, and all based on a conviction of the revelation of God in history. As this was a revelation of God *in history*, the Bible's embeddedness in Hebrew thought had to be taken seriously as did its message about a God who acted.[5] This movement attempted to overcome what had become a separation between biblical studies and theological

---

3. Wilkinson, "Activity of God."
4. Barth, *Word of God and the Word of Man*; *Epistle to the Romans*.
5. G. Wright, *God Who Acts*.

thinking that had arisen in the nineteenth century. Biblical studies had developed a primary interest in the sources, forms, and reception of biblical texts, while theology had become dominated by philosophical considerations.[6] Biblical theology attempted to bring the Bible back to the center of theological discourse.[7]

The movement was attacked on several fronts, but in particular how it was reading and understanding the biblical text in relationship to the miraculous in history. Langdon Gilkey built on earlier arguments of Branton and King to point to a fundamental problem in the biblical theology movement, namely what was meant by the mighty works of God in history.[8] The biblical theology movement had spoken of salvation history, but how was that related to the historical nature of biblical events? Did some events actually happen or were they just the interpretation of the biblical writers? Many within the movement would speak about the historical nature of biblical events but then see the biblical descriptions of them as metaphorical. For example, the call of Moses was historical, but the burning bush was a figure of speech.[9] Thus, it was "an uneasy dualism" to speak of God as acting and speaking, but then ignore the miraculous events that were so much part of the biblical record.[10] This was followed by James Barr, who agreed that the movement's use of history was selective and ambiguous and the rejection of the more supernatural dimensions of the narrative failed to take the Bible as seriously as it claimed.[11]

As a movement, biblical theology was further questioned over the modes of unity within the Bible and its conception of revelation, leading Brevard Childs to speak of a crisis within proposals for new directions.[12] The next few decades showed the continuation of attempts to hold together historical biblical research with systematic theology. But the challenge was summarized by Barr when he argued that we "cannot retreat from the

---

6. Reynolds et al., *Reconsidering the Relationship.*

7. Brunner, *Divine-Human Encounter; Revelation and Reason*; Dodd, *Present Task in New Testament Studies*; Rowley, *Unity of the Bible*; Cullmann, *Christ and Time*; Anderson, *Unfolding Drama of the Bible.*

8. Gilkey, "Cosmology, Ontology," 195. See also Branton, "Our Present Situation in Biblical Theology," 12–13; King, "Some Ambiguities in Biblical Theology," 95.

9. Dorrien, "Modernism as a Theological Problem," 64–94.

10. Gilkey, *Naming the Whirlwind*, 91.

11. Barr, "Revelation Through History," 193–205.

12. Childs, *Biblical Theology in Crisis.*

modern world into a biblical myth."[13] Now in one sense, Barr's critique embraces the importance of the historical critical method, but it also stresses the relationship with the modern world of science. Indeed, the central question of how God acts in not merely a general question but also concerns the particular signs and wonders claimed in the biblical text.

The exploration of biblical theology has been well represented in the names of previous Didsbury Lecturers, including James Dunn, Richard Bauckham, and N. T. Wright. But few have engaged the scientific questions. The exception is Wright, whose work on the bodily resurrection of Jesus has recognized the importance of questions raised by science for theology and, indeed, the mission of a God who acts in the particular.[14]

2.1.2 The Problem of Evil

Of course, the question of how God works within a world described by science comes nowhere near the depth and emotional impact of the problem of evil. The attempt to give a short, simple, and coherent answer to such a question has been at the center of the problem of evil, and a vast, complex, and diverse body of theological literature has arisen concerning it.[15] How can a loving, good, and omnipotent God allow evil within the universe? It has been a powerful argument against Christian faith, and it has encouraged a number of apologetic responses.[16] For example, John Hick proposed that for God to create a world in which morally significant agents could exist, it had to be a world that contained the possibility of real suffering and in which the divine presence was somewhat hidden. Such a world was a vale of "soul making." But all responses to the problem of evil are met with counter-challenges. In Hick's case, many felt it ran aground not on the existence of evil but its scale, both in the natural world and in human experience.[17]

---

13. Barr, "Theological Case Against Biblical Theology," 3–19.

14. N. T. Wright, *Resurrection of the Son of God*; Wright, "Can a Scientist Believe?"

15. Adams and Adams, *Problem of Evil*; Inwagen, *Problem of Evil*; Davies, *Reality of God and the Problem of Evil*; Hebblethwaite, *Problem of Evil*; Søvik, *Problem of Evil and the Power of God*; McBrayer, *Blackwell Companion to the Problem of Evil*; Grebe and Grössl, *T&T Clark Handbook of Suffering*; Trakakis, *Problem of Evil*; C. Wright, *Creation, God, and Humanity*.

16. Loftus, *Christian Delusion*.

17. Geivett, *Evil and the Evidence for God*; Frances, *Gratuitous Suffering*.

The problem of evil is thus complex. First, it is a recognition of the depth and breadth of suffering. This is symbolized in the scale and injustice of the Holocaust, from the roots of antisemitism through to the horrors of the gas chambers. In the non-human world, the scale of the five mass extinction events within the evolutionary development of biological life on Earth—one of which included the dinosaur extinction some sixty-five million years ago—is staggering.[18] In a mass extinction, at least 75 percent of species go extinct within a relatively short period of time. Second, the definition of evil is itself not straightforward. It is an all-encompassing term that can include all pain and suffering. But as Hick was right in pointing out, some pain and suffering is necessary for learning, growth, and development. So, is evil characterized by excess of pain and injustice? And is evil about directed suffering or about the lack of action when suffering could be avoided or alleviated?[19]

The specific response of Christian theology has been interesting. It seems that much work has been done within the Christian tradition of philosophical theology, which has often tended to classical arguments about the nature of omnipotence. But a more authentic Christian response is to supplement these arguments with specific engagement with biblical texts and examples of suffering. This move is good to see in contemporary theology.[20] Much of this work demonstrates "science-engaged theology."[21] Perry and Leidenhag have argued that science and theology are not monolithic distinct lenses. Rather, authentic engagement comes from the way specific scientific and theological disciplines ask questions of each other. Here the stress is on the importance of doing theology well by listening to and engaging with empirical science.[22] Its fruitfulness can be seen in the work of Polkinghorne and many others. But while a recognition of specific

---

18. Bailey et al., "Can Episodic Comet Showers Explain"; Ritchie "There Have Been Five Mass Extinctions."

19. Singer, "Concept of Evil."

20. Blocher, *Evil and the Cross*; Higton, *Deliver Us*; Swinton, *Raging with Compassion*; Surin, *Turnings of Darkness and Light*; Davies, *Reality of God and the Problem of Evil*; Keltz, *Bringing Good Even Out of Evil*; Luy et al., *Evil and Creation*; Rosenberg, *Finding Ourselves After Darwin*; Russell et al., *Evolutionary and Molecular Biology*; Kilby and Davies, *Suffering and the Christian Life*; Southgate, *Groaning of Creation*; Stump, *Image of God*; Creegan, *Animal Suffering and the Problem of Evil*; Schneider, *Animal Suffering and the Darwinian Problem of Evil*; Osborn, *Death Before the Fall*; Dahl, *Problem of Job and the Problem of Evil*.

21. See Perry and Leidenhag, "What Is Science-Engaged Theology?"

22. Perry and Leidenhag, "What Is Science Engaged Theology?," 252.

scientific issues can aid insight, one must say the same for theological insights and the formational history of faith communities. This is of course seen the most in Jewish discussions of evil in the light of the Holocaust. Christian engagement has often been with doctrines, such as creation and fall. While this is essential, I want to suggest that science-engaged theology in the mainstream Christian tradition has to put the life, death, and resurrection of Jesus at the heart of its response to the problem of evil.

Yet as we shall see, the problem of evil has led to an influential reassessment of what God can do and what God wills to do in the physical universe. In this it has interacted in various ways with the scientific model of the world that we considered in the first lecture.[23]

2.2 Models of Providence

I have found it helpful in discussing providence to focus on the picture of God that is given in different ways of thinking about how God can or cannot work in the world. I wish to consider seven such models of God's providence. These models are not exhaustive, but each offers something.

2.2.1 The "Working in the Mind" God

In 1941 Rudolf Bultmann published an influential essay entitled "New Testament and Mythology: The Problem of Demythologizing the New Testament Message." In it he argued:

> We cannot use electric lights and radios and in the event of illness avail ourselves of modern medical and clinical means and at the same time believe in the spirit and wonder world of the New Testament. And if we suppose that we can do so ourselves, we must be clear that we can represent this as the attitude of Christian faith only by making the Christian proclamation unintelligible and impossible for our contemporaries.[24]

The concern with the scientific picture of the world as a dialogue partner in interpreting the New Testament and in communicating the gospel is

---

23. Some groundbreaking work in this area was done by Robert Russell and colleagues in Russell et al., *Quantum Cosmology and the Laws of Nature*; Russell et al., *Neuroscience and the Person*; Russell et al., *Chaos and Complexity*; Russell et al., *Evolutionary and Molecular Biology*.

24. Bultmann, *New Testament and Mythology*, 4–5.

controversial and has come under heavy criticism. Critics have argued that Bultmann allows science to be the final arbiter of interpretation, which not only misrepresents the biblical documents but also privileges such science above all other worldviews.[25]

Now for Bultmann, this is an over-simplification of the content and intention of his program of demythologization.[26] There was a sense that the pre-scientific cosmological myths of the biblical world could not be taken seriously in the modern world. But previous attempts by biblical scholars to purge this element had gone too far, losing the centrality of the gospel, the proclamation that God had acted decisively in the event of Jesus. In fact, demythologizing is not about simply updating the message of the gospel so it aligns with modern science, it is about recognizing something deeper, that is, "the hiddenness and transcendence of divine action" rather than seeking "God's act in the sphere of what is worldly."[27] Supernatural acts and God cannot simply be described in immanent terms.

Now, while this is far more than simply using science to interpret biblical accounts, Bultmann's thinking is shaped by the predictable and picturable Newtonian worldview:

> The idea of wonder as miracle has become almost impossible for us today because we understand the processes of nature as governed by law. Wonder, as miracle, is therefore a violation of the conformity to law which governs all nature, and for us today this idea is no longer tenable.[28]

From this perspective, is there a way to talk about the action of God in a manner that does not violate this conformity of the world to the laws of nature?

Here we open the door to an existentialist approach that draws a distinction between the "exterior" world of science and the "interior" world of religion, in that there is a fundamental difference in our knowledge of physical events compared to the God who is known in experience. God does not act in the physical world in any particular physical way but can achieve God's purposes by "acting" within the person of faith as he or she

---

25. Peckruhn, "Rudolf Bultmann," 191–200; Hart, *Beauty of the Infinite*, 22.

26. Congdon, "Demystifying the Program of Demythologizing," 1–23; Congdon, *Mission of Demythologizing*; Ogden, "Bultmann's Project of Demythologization," 156–73.

27. Bultmann, *New Testament and Mythology*, 122.

28. Bultmann, "Question of Wonder," 241.

encounters God's Word. Prayer for the end of a drought will not lead to God making it rain but to the praying person being moved to help.

There is something to commend such a view. There is a strong biblical tradition that recounts stories where the call of an individual or a community becomes the means for change, repentance, or hope. At the end of Matthew 9, Jesus asks his disciples to pray that the Lord would send out workers into the vast harvest field (Matt 9:38). Perhaps Matthew had a wry smile when he records just a few verses later, "these twelve Jesus sent out" (Matt 10:5). The disciples become the answer to their own prayer.

Further, God cannot be simply seen as agent who is treated as an object or cause confined by the physical world. Certainly, the biblical accounts do not see God as a superhero, akin to a human being with special powers or an alien from another part of the universe. Bultmann is right that the biblical stories see God's relationship with the universe in a far more profound way.

However, this view of God working in the mind of the human agent as distinct from interacting with the physical world has some problems. First, can such a fundamental distinction be made? Even a model of God changing a person's mind implies some particular interaction of God with the physical world. Second, does such a view really make sense of the biblical story? Is God's work confined by only working through human agents?

While Bultmann's motivation to make the Christian faith comprehensible is commendable, he falls into the trap of many fellow theologians in having a Newtonian view of the world. In the predictable and picturable mechanistic world, God cannot have space for agency. Yet in the 1940s when Bultmann was talking about understanding light bulbs, science had already moved on in ways that we saw in the first lecture, not least in our understanding of light!

2.2.2 The "Sit Back and Watch" God

Charles Taylor argued in his widely read *A Secular Age* that the move away from a recognition of and openness toward the transcendent to an exclusive focus on the human in contemporary culture was due to the influence of deism.[29] This belief in the ability of the human to find new moral sources within human community rather than in a revealed religion of miracles and mystery was at the heart of deism, even if we need to recognize that

---

29. Taylor, *Secular Age*, 256.

it is an intellectual movement with a complex historical development and much debate over whether certain thinkers would have owned its title or not.[30] It emerged with force during the Enlightenment with a number of motives forming it.

First was a recognition of the problem of different faith communities with differing and competing views of God. A solution to this was the belief that there was an original, pure, simple, and rational belief in God that had been corrupted by different religious institutions. Second, human reason was the only valid way to work out not just the nature of the world but also the nature of God. This meant, third, that religious texts and religious authorities who claimed the power to mediate knowledge were to be rejected. Or, if not rejected completely, only revealed truth that could be validated through human reason could be accepted. Fourth, as John Locke argued in his *Essay Concerning Human Understanding* (1690), there were no universally accepted innate ideas, and therefore, as Matthew Tindal's *Christianity as Old as the Creation* (1730) would go on to suggest, all arguments should be constructed on reason and our experience of the natural world.

This emphasis on reason and the observation of the natural world gave a fertile ground for the growth of the argument from design. Reason was a gift from God, and the clockwork nature of the world led to the belief that it was created by God. But the clockwork view also meant that the miraculous stories of the Bible were to be rejected, thus leading to a view of God who set the clock in motion in the original creation but then let it develop without intervention. This latter notion has become the popular definition of deism.[31]

This move away from revealed religion to the design argument, energized by deism, was a moment of crucial importance to Christian theological and attempted apologetic engagement with the world. It seemed to offer much in a universal rational proof of the existence of God unencumbered by the complexities of religious texts and power-hungry religious institutions, but as we have seen, it raised numerous problems at the same time. One of its fiercest critics was the Scottish philosopher David Hume, who we will return to in the next lecture, for he was equally ferocious about miracles.[32] But Hume's critique of the design argument argued that reason

---

30. Bristow, "Enlightenment"; Orr, *English Deism*; Wigelsworth, *Deism in Enlightenment England*; Harper, *Multiverse Deism*; Hudson, *Atheism and Deism Revalued*.

31. Peters, "Models of God," 51–52; Shollenberger, *God and His Coexistent Relations*.

32. Yoder, *Hume on God*.

could not establish a solid foundation for belief in a Christian God. While you could observe order and beauty in the world, you also observed suffering and evil. What did this mean for the nature of God? And even a sympathetic attitude to the logic of the design argument meant that at best all you might say is that *something* may have created the universe, but that could be a demiurge rather than the all-powerful and all loving God claimed by Christian theists.

Now while Taylor may argue that deism has led to a rejection of transcendence in the natural world, it also influenced a view of God within Christian theology, which wanted to take seriously both the mechanistic view of the world and the problem of evil. Indeed, this has been a feature of the shape of mission and ministry in many Western churches.[33]

An example of that is Maurice Wiles's Bampton Lectures, published as *God's Action in the World*. This was published when I was a theology undergraduate and was set reading. Rather cheekily, we often referred to it as "God's Inaction in the World."

Wiles argues that God's action is limited to the one great single act that caused and keeps the universe in being. In this sense it is not deism, as God continues to sustain the world. However, it comes close to deism in its rejection of God's particular action in the world and its dismissal of the biblical record of miracles.

His analogy is that of an improvised drama. The author gives basic characters and the setting. The resulting drama may follow the intention of the author, but the actors have freedom to determine their own outcome. God becomes almost a theatre impresario who provides the finance and venue for a production but then sits back and watches what develops without interfering. It is an act that allows radical freedom to human creatures and indeed radical self-limitation on God's part. Thus, for Wiles, providence becomes a kind of teleological insight into the general physical process that interprets religious experience in retrospect. For example, conversion is not to be understood as God forming a particular relationship with an individual but is simply an individual recognizing God's action in bringing the world into being.

Again, there is much to commend in such a picture. If God is at work in the creation and sustaining of the world, then part of its expression will certainly be found in the universality, reliability, and beauty of the laws of nature.

---

33. Horton, *Christless Christianity*.

The Newtonian clockwork universe models this in a simple way. In this sense, God must have a consistent rather than fitful relationship with creation.

Here a response to the problem of evil is powerful. Evil becomes the risk taken by God in allowing freedom to creatures within a physical lawful environment. God simply cannot intervene in the world, even if God is moved by compassion. Wiles demonstrates how the clockwork universe and the problem of evil come together to give a particular model of God.

However, there are several weaknesses. First, you will be getting tired of me saying here is another theologian who is decades if not centuries behind on the scientific picture of the universe. Wiles feels constrained by Newton's clockwork view of the cosmos, but the universe is much more supple and subtle than Newton realized. Now that is not to say that the laws of physics do exhibit universality, reliability, and beauty, but that does not mean that due to the science God's agency in the world is ruled out.

Second, a God who does nothing particular in the universe makes it difficult to see how God can be spoken of in terms of personal relationships.[34] The theater owner who is never seen or heard is no different from a faceless corporate institution who may be paying the costs of the theater as a tax write off.

Third, and most importantly, such a picture of God has little connection with the Christian claim of a God who becomes incarnate and raises Jesus from the dead. It is striking that Wiles is very sensitive to this point. In fact, he spends some considerable time arguing that there is no historical event of a bodily resurrection of Jesus. While he is far from deism in seeing God sustaining the world, on the dismissal of the miraculous events of the Bible he is very close.

2.2.3 The "Persuasive" God

Process theology has also been a movement that has tried to think about God's action in the world in light of the importance of the problem of evil and a scientific understanding of the world. Not wanting to be constrained by the Newtonian mechanistic universe, it found a resource in the philosophy of Alfred North Whitehead (1861–1947) and Charles Hartshorne (1897–2000).

This philosophy perhaps was more influenced by the dynamic nature of evolution rather than more static Newtonian picture. It built its

---

34. White, *Fall of a Sparrow*.

metaphysics of reality not on objects but on events, stressing the importance of change and time. In this, *relation* was key. While Whitehead's *Process and Reality* gave the name process theology, his preferred expression was "the philosophy of organism."[35]

It is important to recognize that this was primarily a philosophical understanding of the world onto which foundation theologians found an opportunity to think about God in a different way. Unlike classical theism, which sees God as unchanging and unaffected by the world or the passage of time, process theology sees God as completely engaged with and changed by time and the world.

Thus, shaped by the philosophy of organism rather than the Newtonian clock, process theology uses an analogy between God's action and our experience as agents and attempts to proceed by assimilating the nature of the universe to our nature. The suggestion was that each event in the universe has a psychic pole and a material pole, and God works as an agent at the subjective level, exercising power by persuasion or lure rather than coercion.

This dual nature of reality is also seen here in God. God's classical attributes of being eternal, immutable, and impassible are seen as only part of God's nature. This eternal pole is complemented by a temporal pole which changes in relation with a changing world. This temporal pole is at the heart of God's nature, along with the eternal pole, and both are equally important.

The attraction of this view is that God does not intervene directly with the physical world. Rather God is able to lure the physical while interacting with the "spiritual." Here the problem of evil is answered by questioning or modifying God's omnipotence. Hartshorne reacts against "the *tyrant* ideal of power" in classical theism, arguing that God works *in relationship with* natural processes and human agents rather than by simply controlling them.[36] Every being, including God, acts persuasively in determining process and change.

Process theology became a popular theological movement with a highpoint in the 1960s and 1970s.[37] It appealed to a number of Wesleyan theologians and was also favored by one of the pioneers of theology and

---

35. See Whitehead, *Process and Reality*; Viney, "Process Theism"; Dombrowski, *Whitehead's Religious Thought*.

36. Hartshorne, *Omnipotence and Other Theological Mistakes*, 11.

37. Cobb and Griffin, *Process Theology*; Pailin, *God and the Processes of Reality*; Clayton, *Problem of God in Modern Thought*; Faber, *Becoming of God*; Leidenhag, *Minding Creation*; Nash, *Process Theology*.

the physical sciences, Ian Barbour.[38] For the Wesleyans, the reality of free will fit well with this process approach. It also gave a strong response to the problem of evil, God creating a world where the risk of evil is real through the gift of freedom.

Yet process theology has had a wide variety of critiques.[39] There are questions whether the classical attributes of God are too far undermined alongside worries about God's creativity and Trinitarian nature. At an even more fundamental level lies the question of whether the basic metaphysics of process thought can be justified. There is no evidence that a scientist might be able to examine that the physical world has such a nature. Of course, the point is that process theology is based on a philosophical choice rather than scientific insight. But to the physical scientist the thought seems odd that even primitive objects such as quarks have an ability to select or influence outcomes in a psychic sense.

In terms of God's action in the world, many have argued that it is difficult to see how God can do anything of importance at such a level, suggesting that the God of process theology is more to be pitied than worshipped.[40] Is God reduced to a passive deity like Wiles's creator? David Basinger has argued that sometimes coercion needs to be used in response to a moral imperative and therefore a God who possesses only persuasive power is less than a God who possesses both coercive and persuasive power.[41] In response to Basinger, Viney maintains that in order to attribute both forms of power to God, it seems to require that God have the power to violate the laws of nature, contravening the very laws that God imposed in the first place.

Nevertheless, process theology opened up a theological space for the development of a more complex understanding of God's relationship with time and the physical processes of the universe. Paul Fiddes welcomes the insight of the "responsiveness and resistance" of creation to the Spirit of God.[42]

---

38. Barbour, *When Science Meets Religion*.

39. Neville, *Creativity and God*; Orr, *Classical Response to Relational Theism*; Truesdale, *God Reconsidered*; Boyd, *Trinity and Process*; Suchocki, *Trinity in Process*; Burrell, "Does Process Theology Rest on a Mistake?"; Case-Winters, *God's Power*.

40. See, for example, Gunton, *Becoming amid Being*; Abraham, *Divine Agency and Divine Action*.

41. Basinger, *Divine Power in Process Theism*.

42. Fiddes, "Process Theology."

2.2.4 The "Embodied" God

"Panentheism" uses an analogy between God's action and our action by comparing God's action in the world to our action in our bodies. For some of them, the world can be thought of as something like "the body of God."[43] By seeing the organic relatedness of the world and God, process theology had suggested that in some sense the world is "part" of God. But panentheism, a word invented by Karl Krause (1781–1832), suggests that the world exists *within* God. This differs from pantheism, where the world is the same as God, and from classical theism where the world is in some sense "external" to God.

Panentheism thus can hold both divine transcendence and immanence. God is greater than the world but still intimately connected with the world, and the world can influence God.

Panentheism has been deployed to understand God not just in the Christian tradition but also in other faith communities. It has been attractive to a number of leading thinkers in the engagement of science and theology, such as Arthur Peacocke and Philip Clayton. Peacocke, from his perspective as a biologist, rejected the Newtonian description of the world as mechanistic and reducible to its smallest constituent parts. He saw emergent levels of relationship and novelty coming out of a world of both complexity and unity. Relating this to God, Peacocke likewise rejects any model of God intervening from outside of the natural world. God is continuously at work through the creativity of the natural order, that is, God working not from the outside but from the inside. The model of a fetus in the mother's womb gives a sense of this. God is involved in sustaining the evolution of complexity from the inside while being greater than the universe.[44]

Clayton is also attracted to seeing God's action in the world from the inside rather than the outside. God is the source and sustainer of the physical laws and remains in a relationship of interdependence with the universe while being distinct from the universe. Here there is an echo of process theology in a dual nature of God.[45] Clayton is a stronger advocate of a Trinitarian understanding than Peacocke. Indeed, the relationship of

---

43. Culp, "Panentheism"; Biernacki, *Panentheism Across the World's Traditions*.
44. Peacocke, *Creation and the World of Science*; "Emergence, Mind, and Divine Action"; *Paths from Science Towards God*; *Theology for a Scientific Age*.
45. Clayton, "Panentheism in Metaphysical and Scientific Perspective."

God and the universe is analogous to the interdependence and coinherence of the persons of the Trinity.[46]

Panentheism has also been advocated by a number of feminist theologians who have found in it a way to go beyond the dualism of an evil material world and a good spiritual one that so infected much Western conceptions of God and the world. Using models of fetus and mother as well as midwifery, panentheism affirms the goodness of the physical and the intimate involvement of God in every part of the world.[47] In fact, some have gone further and, in the words of Grace Jantzen, see the world as God's body.[48] Thus, God can act on any part of the world in a way similar to our action on our bodies.

Such an approach has many strengths. It holds together immanence and transcendence in a way that avoids both pantheism and a deistic God completely external to the universe. It takes contemporary science seriously in seeing beyond the Newtonian clockwork model and sees God at work within the laws of nature. This is a God of intimate relationship, and the physicality of the world is affirmed rather than demonized.

However, several problems have been raised.[49] First, do we understand enough about human embodiment to use such an analogy? And how do we work in our own bodies beyond sustaining the processes of life? In such a model, can God do anything in particular? Here Clayton and others point to the idea of top-down causation, which they argue we see in the mind-brain relationship. The classic example of this is how the learning of "The Knowledge" by London taxi drivers has led to a measurable enlargement of part of the brain.[50] So, it is argued we can work at a physical level within our own bodies to cause change.

That, however, has not been convincing to all. Joanna Leidenhag and Mikael Leidenhag have argued that the absence of ontological difference between God and the universe on this model means that it is difficult to see or identify God's causal influence on the world.[51]

Further, panentheism has another vulnerability, one related to the problem of evil. If God is so intimately involved in every part of the world,

---

46. Clayton, "Panentheist Internalism."

47. Frankenberry, "Classical Theism, Panentheism"; Schaab, "Midwifery as a Model"; Jantzen, *Becoming Divine*; McFague, *Body of God*; *Models of God*.

48. Jantzen, *God's World, God's Body*.

49. Cooper, *Panentheism*; Tabaczek, *Divine Action and Emergence*.

50. Maguire et al., "Navigation-Related Structural Change."

51. Leidenhag, "Is Panentheism Naturalistic"; "Critique of Emergent Theologies."

is God therefore responsible for all the evil generated within it?[52] Oord responds to this challenge by arguing that God's love is uncontrolling, creating a world with the *possibility* of evil but *not causing* evil.[53]

Evil is not only a problem for a Christian theology of origins but also for a Christian theology of its eventual defeat. In panentheism, can God in any way ultimately triumph over evil?

Third, if the universe is in some way God's "body," then does God become vulnerable as the universe changes with time? The analogy is very good at 13.8 billion years, when the universe has order and discernible structure, but it is totally inappropriate when in its early history the universe is a quark soup or when in its far future all structure, such as stars and galaxies, is being ripped apart by its accelerated expansion.[54] And if the universe is God's "body," then what was God like before the Big Bang, before God had such a body?

Fourth, such an analogy sees the nature of the physical world as an organism having unity to its overall structure. But the universe is just too subtle to fit the picture. In some senses it shows "organism" qualities, in other senses "mechanistic" qualities, and in other senses "chaotic" qualities, of which saw in lecture 1. It is a subtle admixture of many things.

Fifth, it can be argued that panentheism threatens God's otherness and freedom but also compromises the world's freedom to be itself.

2.2.5 The "Open" God

Process theism and panentheism gave rise in part to a new theological movement that has become known as open theology. In fact, Hartshorne had referred to the "openness of God" as early as 1963, but it became a distinct movement in the last two decades of the twentieth century due to a development of the idea of kenosis, an engagement with certain biblical narratives, and some of the scientific developments we reviewed earlier.

Since the work of Vanstone and Moltmann, it has become fashionable in some quarters of mainstream theology to see God's creative love always accompanied by vulnerability.[55] In God's kenosis, God self-limits, giving

---

52. Leidenhag, "Critique of Emergent Theologies," 879.

53. Oord, *Uncontrolling Love of God*.

54. Wilkinson and Hutchings, *God, Stephen Hawking and the Multiverse*; Wilkinson, *Christian Eschatology and the Physical Universe*.

55. Vanstone, *Love's Endeavour, Love's Expense*; Moltmann, *God in Creation*.

to humans and to the universe a degree of freedom to explore their and its own potentiality. God creates through an evolutionary process that includes chance in order to give human beings the possibility of development with the consequence of the risk of suffering.[56]

Flowing into this were some of the streams of thinking we have outlined previously. Jürgen Moltmann echoed panentheism by seeing, both in creation and eschatology, life being taken into the life of the Trinitarian God.[57] In this God does not need to create but chooses to create in love by limiting his presence and power to make space for creation. Kenosis is thus seen not only in the emptying and self-limiting of God in becoming incarnate in Jesus but also as being at the heart of all creation. On this Clayton is very similar.[58] Indeed, in some senses it is difficult to make too sharp a distinction between process theology, panentheism, and the emergence of open theology. All are attempting to find models to represent immanence, transcendence, and kenosis, allowing radical freedom to human creatures and, indeed, radical self-limitation on God's part.[59] The difference is largely whether the limitation on God is due to God's fundamental nature or whether it is an act of self-limitation. In the midst of this would be Oord's concept of essential kenosis, where he argues that the emptying of divine attributes is based on divine nature rather than divine will.[60]

These themes found resonance among certain evangelical scholars who argued for a fresh emphasis on the God of the Bible, who was revealed in the primacy of self-giving love, which itself was accompanied by vulnerability.[61] It provoked a serious and at times bitter controversy among evangelicals, not least between those with Wesleyan/Arminian views of providence and those with Calvinist views.[62] The debate was fuelled by a political struggle within evangelicalism between reformed movements

---

56. Brown, *Divine Humanity*; Hinshaw and Behr, *Thriving in the Face of Mortality*; Nimmo and Johnson, *Kenosis*; Oord, *Uncontrolling Love of God*.

57. Moltmann, *Coming of God*; *God in Creation*; *Trinity and the Kingdom of God*.

58. Clayton, "Kenotic Trinitarian Panentheism."

59. Cobb and Pinnock, *Searching for an Adequate God*.

60. Oord, *Uncontrolling Love of God*, 158–66.

61. Sanders, *God Who Risks*; Pinnock et al., *Openness of God*; Pinnock, *Most Moved Mover*; Hall and Sanders, *Does God Have a Future?*; Hasker, *Providence, Evil*.

62. Long and Kalantzis, *Sovereignty of God Debate*; Hasker et al., *God in an Open Universe*; Bray, *Personal God*; Helm, *Providence of God*; Carson, *Gagging of God*.

influenced by Calvinist theologies and the growth of more Arminian Pentecostal and charismatic traditions, which acknowledge a debt to Wesley.[63]

At the heart of the controversy was American theologian Clark Pinnock. Pinnock and John Sanders faced a vote to be expelled from the Evangelical Theological Society on this issue, but the required two thirds majority was not reached. Pinnock argued that traditional theism championed by Calvinism's view of an all-controlling sovereignty was developed primarily from Greek philosophy and is profoundly unbiblical, thus the God we encounter is "manipulative, futureless, motionless, remote, isolated." In contrast, the Bible uses images of God as a free personal agent who acts in love, co-operates with people, and responds to prayer.[64] God creates a world where the future is not yet completely settled and takes seriously our response. Pinnock speaks of the "most moved mover" in contrast to the "unmoved mover" of classical theism. He argues that this understanding of the providence of God has significant practical consequences in the areas of prayer and lifestyle.

There is some similarity here with process theism. Freewill is key, arguing that God does not override creaturely freedom and takes such freedom seriously in the development of the future. This means that the future in some respects is yet to be determined, that it is open. God is in relationship with human beings, so prayer really makes a difference. But for other evangelicals, this idea of the openness of the future is troubling. Does it deny God's omnipotence and God's knowledge of the future? Are there certain things that even God does not know about the future? Does this compromise God's omniscience and undermine God's simplicity in the sense that God changes with time?

Pinnock suggests that it does indeed lead to some different understandings of classical theological terms:

> God's unity will not be viewed as mathematical oneness but as a unity that includes diversity; God's steadfastness will not be seen as a deadening immutability but constancy of character that includes change; God's power will not be seen as raw omnipotence but as the sovereignty of love whose strength is revealed in weakness; and

---

63. Cross, "Rich Feast of Theology," 30–31; Stone and Oord, *Thy Nature and Thy Name Is Love*.

64. Pinnock, *Most Moved Mover*.

> God's omniscience will not be seen as know-it-all but as a wisdom which shapes the future in dialogue with creatures.[65]

Openness theologians want to depart from process theology here. First, they claim to be motivated more by Scripture than by philosophy. Second, there is a greater stress on God's transcendence, defending *creatio ex nihilo*, the possibility of miracles, and the ultimate triumph of God over evil. In process theology God is limited to exercising influence only by persuasive power, and that is in the nature of things rather than freewill choice.

While pointing out a number of weaknesses, Fackre nevertheless sees the strengths of the openness view as highlighting God's suffering love, taking seriously the biblical narrative, and giving reality to the experience of daily prayer.[66] I would agree with this.

Yet as I have argued elsewhere, we must be careful not to go too far.[67] Pinnock emphasizes that open theology recognizes the primacy of Scripture. It is the case that the Bible does take God responding to prayer seriously and emphasizes the importance of human freewill, not least in matters of sin and salvation. Yet, Scripture is really quite messy! For example, Pinnock claims that the parable of the prodigal son (Luke 15:11–32) "dramatizes the truth of the open view of God," emphasizing the waiting Father who does not override the son's decision to go to a far country and then return.[68] But we need to note that Luke joins this parable with two other parables that "dramatize" God as taking the initiative in seeking a lost sheep and a lost coin (Luke 15:1–10). Here God's sovereignty in salvation is in dramatic tension with the gift of freedom. This neglect of emphasis on God's initiative also surfaces in Pinnock's description of a "bilateral covenant" in the Old Testament between God and his people. Yet the nature of the covenant depended on God's free act of grace and then Israel's response in the obligations of grace.

This becomes more of a problem for the openness view when it comes to the long-term future. Its biblical emphasis wants to reflect the anticipated victory of good over evil, but it is difficult to see how this might happen. Further, there is virtually no engagement with the major biblical themes of a new heaven and new earth. Pinnock does use the analogy of God as the "master chess player." God is the consummate guide, allowing

---

65. Pinnock, *Most Moved Mover*, 27.
66. Fackre, "Review."
67. Wilkinson, *When I Pray*.
68. Pinnock, *Most Moved Mover*, 4.

A Science-Shaped God?

both freedom to the other person involved in the game and yet able to bring about ultimate victory. But does such an analogy represent genuine openness? The struggle to find an adequate picture shows the limits of the openness view in the light of God's ultimate purpose.

This also illustrates an inherent problem in philosophical theology. The temptation is to go to one extreme or another—either the future is completely open or the future is entirely determined by God. That temptation is to try and articulate a model of God's relationship with the universe that is simple to understand in human terms. It may be that no one model is adequate.

Yet openness theology does find some scientific support in the openness of the scientific description of the world that we noted in the first lecture.[69] The unpredictability of quantum theory at the micro level and chaos at the macro level suggests for some a genuine openness to the future in the physical world.

John Polkinghorne, as a critical realist, argued that epistemology and ontology need to be closely linked. Therefore, our limitations in making predictions about the future indicated an ontologically-undetermined future. He saw this especially in chaotic systems, as quantum systems encounter the measurement problem (that is, the question of how the microworld actually leads to changes in the everyday world).[70] This scientific insight coupled with kenosis meant that God gives the gift of freedom to the process of the world, to human beings, and to God's own exercise of particular agency within the world. In chaotic physical systems, the action of God remains hidden but can make changes in the everyday world. That the universe is open to the future, unpredictable, and undetermined, allows it to become the "space" both for human freedom and for a free-process defense for natural evil. Just as the freewill defense to the problem of evil stressed the consequences of bad choices by human beings, so, too, the physical processes of the universe had some God-given freedom. In exploring that potentiality, the consequences could be both helpful and detrimental to human experience. Providence therefore becomes a subtle interaction between our freedom, the freedom inherent in the physical nature of the universe, and God's freedom to act. Indeed, if there is room in the physical world for our own exercise of free will, then surely God must enjoy similar room.

---

69. Hasker et al., *God in an Open Universe*; Oord, *Creation Made Free*; *Defining Love*.
70. See, e.g., Polkinghorne, *Science and Providence*; *Work of Love*.

How Does God Act in the World?

The attractiveness of Polkinghorne's approach is that it takes much more seriously the post-Newtonian view of the world. In addition, chaotic systems have a great advantage over quantum systems in that their effects are felt at the everyday level. God is at work in the flexibility of these seemingly open systems as well as being the ground of law. God's particular activity is real, but it is hidden. Polkinghorne has gone beyond kenotic and openness theology in many of the approaches above by locating God's action within specific physical systems. Therefore, is it right to pray for rain? Yes, it is, according to Polkinghorne. This is because the weather system is a chaotic system showing this openness to the future. Is it right to pray for summer to come before spring? The answer is no, for the seasons are determined by the simple non-chaotic system of the Earth's rotation about the Sun.

In response, we may raise a number of questions. First, does chaos imply just a limitation on our knowledge rather than a genuine ontological openness in the universe itself? Polkinghorne's defense is to say that there comes an inherent limit to predicting chaotic system by the time you need to specify the initial conditions at the level of quantum theory and its uncertainty and by needing a computer to solve the equations which is bigger than the universe itself. Of course, we might not know the future but is an infinite God limited in this way? God may know the future even if we cannot. As Ian Stewart noted, "If God played dice he would win!"[71]

Second, should God be confined to such "gaps" of scientific prediction? It is important to note that the "gaps" referred to here are not the same as in the "God of the gaps" referred to earlier. God of the gaps is a critique for inserting God as an easy answer when science has not progressed sufficiently in its understanding. Rather, Polkinghorne is suggesting that there are ontological gaps in knowing the future state of a system which are exposed by scientific theory. The question theologically here is whether God's activity is so self-limited to chaotic systems and in such a way that it is hidden. While Polkinghorne is explicit that part of God's work is the regular sustaining of the laws of physics, the danger of the hiddenness of God's particular action is that it does not do justice to the biblical record, which suggests that some of God's actions, rather than being hidden, are in fact signs.

---

71. Stewart, *Does God Play Dice?*

2.2.6 The "Double Agency" God

If Polkinghorne suggested that chaos kept the action of God hidden, he nevertheless wanted to identify how God acted within the scientific structure of the world. Rather than describing in scientific terms the causal joint of God's action, Austin Farrer argued that we cannot conceive of God's way of acting in terms of our own, and therefore the causal joint between God's action and ours will always be hidden. For Farrer "the relation of created act to creative Act is inevitably indefinable."[72]

Farrer was seen by many as one of the leading philosophical and theological Anglican voices of the twentieth century.[73] While ranging across many disciplines, from biblical studies to ecclesiology, perhaps his most notable discussion was in the area of providence. For Farrer, as God is far "beyond" this universe and our ability to describe God's actions in terms of this universe, the response to providence is not to try and squeeze it into our scientific view of the world but to live faithful Christian lives in response to it. Thus, he suggested a model of "double agency" where God is the cause of all things rather than a cause alongside other causes in the world. In fact, God is the cause of the acting of created beings, which means that their acts are truly their own, and this means that one can speak of the act of God and the act of the creature not as distinct but inextricably joined.[74] Both God and the creature are simultaneously causing the whole action. Each event in the universe will therefore have a double description, which can be spoken of in terms of the providential action of God and at the same time have a full natural description in the laws of nature or the action of human agents.

This full description in the laws of nature, given by the creative action of God, goes someway in a response to the problem of evil. In discussing earthquakes, for example, Farrer writes: "The will of God expressed in the event is his will for the physical elements in the Earth's crust or under it: his will that they should go on being themselves and acting in accordance with their natures."[75]

---

72. Farrer, *Faith and Speculation*, 170.

73. Curtis, *Hawk Among Sparrows*; Hebblethwaite, *Philosophical Theology of Austin Farrer*; Hebblethwaite and Henderson, *Divine Action*; Hein and Henderson, *Captured by the Crucified*; MacSwain, *Solved by Sacrifice*.

74. Vogel, "Self-Effacing Gardener."

75. Farrer, *Faith and Speculation*, 88.

This is not Farrer's full response to the problem of evil, as he also stresses the importance of God's revelation in Jesus Christ.[76] This is also important for how God is known. Such a view has no place for the design argument: "If it has a gardener, the natural world is a wild garden laid out with so skillful and so self-effacing an informality that the gardener's hand can never be convincingly detected in any single feature."[77]

Such an approach has been followed by others who have vigorously defended a strong view of God's providential guiding of history while at the same time allowing for a complementary description in terms of natural processes. It is interesting to note that this has included leading scientists such as Sir John Houghton and Professor Donald MacKay.[78] Indeed, in an echo of double agency, Houghton argued for a "big enough" God who was able to work out his purposes through scientific processes even if we could not fully understand how God would be able to do it.

Again, this view has some attraction, not least in asking the question whether God's action can ever be understood within the context of this finite world. Yet a number of objections have been raised. The first echoes the joke of Ricky Gervais—that is, is this simply a retreat into mystery? Polkinghorne and Wiles argued that Farrer's double agency does little to help our understanding of how God works in the world. Indeed, that God is causing things in a way that always stays hidden from us begs the question of whether we can use the word at all.[79] The second is whether there is any sense in which the freedom given to the physical processes in the world or human action is real.

2.3 Some Contributions from the Wesleyan Tradition

In this lecture so far, we have surveyed some of the main options on the table in thinking about God's action in the universe, attempting to take seriously biblical theology, the problem of evil, and contemporary scientific and philosophical views of the world. Throughout these lectures we have noted Walter Wink's insight that "people with an attenuated sense of what is possible will bring that conviction to the Bible and diminish it by the

---

76. Oliver, "Theodicy of Austin Farrer."
77. Farrer, *Faith and Speculation*, 74.
78. Houghton, *Search for God*; MacKay, *Science, Chance and Providence*.
79. Wiles, "Farrer's Concept of Double Agency"; Polkinghorne, *Science and Providence*, 15–16.

poverty of their own experience."[80] Here we have seen that for scholars such as Wiles and Bultmann, the Newtonian worldview constrains what they think is possible. One cannot underestimate the significance of this. In an influential paper in 1968 Kaufman stated, "We cannot conceive of an event without prior finite causes."[81] Yet by that stage quantum theory had been around for some forty years.

On the other hand, the philosophical insights of process philosophy and scientific insights such as chaos theory have given new possibilities for thinking about providence. In all of this there have been some commonalities, in particular, trying to take seriously both God's action and the problem of evil and to hold together God's transcendence and immanence.

Each of the models has something to offer the wider discussion: Emphasis on God's reliable upholding of the regular patterns of the physical laws; the experience of freedom in human beings and perhaps in the physical process; the difficulty of reducing God's causation to be simply one cause among many within the world; and maintaining the hope that God's love will eventually triumph over evil are all important.

I therefore am not convinced that any one of the above models is a convincing model to explain the complexity of God's action in the world. Rather, I would like to suggest some further insights that come from the Wesleyan tradition. This is perhaps fitting, given that the lectures on which this book is based were hosted in a Nazarene theological college and that my own theological heritage is that of British Methodism.

First, *we need to adopt a theological method that does not aim for simple models.* John Wesley, the founder of the Methodist movement, has been a frustrating figure for later historians and theologians. This has been due to his lack of any articulation of a systematic theology and his display of what seem to be inconsistent beliefs and practices in his ministry. As Randy Maddox has argued, Wesley was a practical theologian, not because he simply dabbled in theology to fit his missional purposes but because he was part of a tradition that took praxis-related theology seriously within particular situations.[82] This raises the question of whether there should be consistency in theological thinking. Maddox suggests that in the modern Western model of systematic theology the concern for consistency was seen as the need for all theological claims to be derived from or subsumed

---

80. Wink, "Write What You See," 6.
81. Kaufman, "On the Meaning of 'Act of God.'"
82. Maddox, "John Wesley—Practical Theologian?"

under a single idea.[83] The pursuit of this single idea often then reduces the complexity of insights from within a particular discipline or often ignores insights from other disciplines. Rather, consistency can arise from a basic "orientating *perspective* or concern that guides their various theological activities."[84] Further, Maddox argues that it is not necessary to have a comprehensive summary of the claims consistent with such a perspective prior to engaging in theological reflection. It is *the search* for consistent expressions in relation to new issues that enlivens a theological perspective.

This is the basis of Wesley's ability to hold together complexity. As Donald English noted, "Wesley's greatest contribution of all was his ability to face seemingly intractable problems and to place them into a creative tension which was not resolved but was lifegiving."[85]

One might also add that Wesley was concerned more with integrity in theological method rather than a rigid systematic expression of doctrine. Much debate in contemporary scholarship has centred on the Wesleyan quadrilateral of Scripture, reason, experience, and tradition, first promoted by Albert Outler.[86] The debate is around how these sources of authority were understood by Wesley and how they are understood now, and further whether Scripture has primacy within it.[87] Yet leaving these debates aside for the moment, the Wesleyan way of holding together experience, reason, Bible, and tradition is extremely fruitful for the theological examination of providence.

Chaos and quantum theory must be taken seriously. They may not provide easy gaps into which one can insert the intervention of God, but they do demolish the mechanistic universe that has so dominated discussions of providence. They remind us also that any model of providence must reflect the varied and complex nature of the universe. There is predictability and unpredictability, and a number of different avenues that God may choose to interact with the universe. At the same time, theology must be serious in its interaction with science but must not be dominated by it. The Methodist quadrilateral is a simple way of challenging any discussion of providence that is overly dominated by either experience, reason, Bible, or tradition.

83. See also Wood, *Vision and Discernment*.
84. Maddox, "John Wesley—Practical Theologian?," 136; "Responsible Grace."
85. English, *From Wesley's Chair*, 91.
86. Outler, "Wesleyan Quadrilateral in Wesley."
87. Gunter et al., *Wesley and the Quadrilateral*; Thorson, *Wesleyan Quadrilateral*; Abraham, "Wesleyan Quadrilateral."

Interestingly, Outler shows a commendable engagement with science in 1968.[88] He begins by considering just how closed nature and history are to the action of God. Rejecting quantum theory as the gap in which God works, he nevertheless uses it to show the limits of science and to make the case that the scientific laws are provisional and descriptive not prescriptive.

It is interesting that the doctrine of providence has often been located in the areas of systematic or philosophical theology. In the past this has often isolated it from scientific insights and indeed the complexity of the biblical material. Further, within those disciplines there has been a tendency to move towards a coherent and simple model of providence. This leads the modern Calvinists into one rigid model, while at the other end of the theological spectrum, God is divested of any power or freedom in order to acquit God in the face of evil.

A Wesleyan contribution would therefore be to resist any attempt to oversimplify the doctrine for the sake of resolving all tensions. Complexity and mystery must be maintained, especially if this is life-giving. Such complexity concerning providence has always been at the heart of Scripture, reason, tradition, and experience. Even a non-Wesleyan such as Calvin explores such complexity when he sees God, the Chaldeans, and Satan as all active in the Chaldeans' attack on Job's shepherds and flock! Further, sometimes the Bible claims that nothing happens that God does not make happen (e.g., Isa 45:7) and sometimes that time and chance have an important part to play (e.g., Eccl 9:11–12).

This difficult tension is a reminder that any one view of providence might be neat and simple in the philosophy textbook but may be far too simplistic to do justice to a complex universe and the God who is beyond that universe. It is an easy trap to look for a simple philosophical or theological system and ignore some of the biblical data or indeed our experience of God's work in our lives.

Second, if the Wesleyan theological approach is primarily about an orientating perspective, what perspective might that be? A major emphasis in recent Wesleyan theology has been the recognition that the theme of new creation is a major component of Wesley's mature theology and indeed may play an integrative role.[89] Maddox has helpfully characterized this "trajectory" in Wesley's theology as moving through new creation from the personal spiritual dimension and the socio-political dimension to the

---

88. See Outler, *Who Trusts in God*.

89. Outler, "New Future for 'Wesley Studies'"; Runyon, *New Creation*.

cosmic dimension.[90] It is clear from the first part of this lecture that the doctrine of providence has largely been centred on the doctrine of creation with little attempt to reflect the importance in Christian tradition of new creation. It is the perspective of the cosmic dimension of new creation that can be brought to the development of any doctrine of providence. Providence must relate to *both* creation and new creation. While the nature of creation will inform providence in terms of God's constant sustaining of the universe and his giving of freedom, the nature of new creation brings questions of God's ongoing purpose and his own freedom into the discussion.

As I have argued elsewhere, biblical passages that focus on new creation emphasize the sovereign act of God, with eschatology understood as the climax of the Creator's work. New creation is only possible because the God of creation is still at work providing new possibilities.[91] Hope for the future is built on an understanding that God the redeemer is the same as God the creator (Isa 65:17–25). Whatever the circumstances, creation is not limited to its own inherent possibilities because the God of creation is still at work. Thus, the sovereignty of God in creation is the basis of hope that God will transform this creation into a new heaven and new earth. The key question for providence is whether this sense of God's overall sovereignty in bringing the story of creation to new creation is given strong enough emphasis. As Richard Bauckham comments:

> A God who is not the transcendent origin of all things but a way of speaking of the immanent creative possibilities of the universe itself cannot be the ground of ultimate hope for the future of creation. Where faith in God the Creator wanes, so inevitably does hope for the resurrection, let alone the new creation of all things.[92]

On the basis of this insight, we need to be careful about models that make God dependent on the universe or subvert God's *ex nihilo* creation. It is only a transcendent creator who can give the hope of new creation for a good but broken world. Models of providence have to take seriously the universe over its entire history rather than just the present state of the universe. Those that picture the universe as God's body work reasonably well with a universe of its present structure, variety, and life but are weak when we look forward to a universe that decays in the futility of a lifeless and

---

90. Maddox, "Nurturing the New Creation."
91. Wilkinson, *Christian Eschatology*; "Accelerating Universe."
92. Bauckham, *Theology of the Book of Revelation*, 51.

unstructured heat death. Models that stress immanence too much at the expense of transcendence face a bleak future in terms of the end of the universe.

Likewise, models that stress God's non-intervention in the universe are presented with interesting questions in terms of the end of the universe. For example, does Wiles take seriously that his model pictures God as sustaining a process that will end in futility? The universe may seem creative and diverse now, giving the human actors freedom to work out the drama as they wish. But what of the time when the universe is tending to destruction? Has God given the actors freedom to work out their own drama in a theatre that is destined for demolition?

The eschatological dimension also questions open views of the future. Many of these views want to reflect eschatological closure in the victory of good over evil, but it is difficult to see how this might happen. As we have seen, in Pinnock's case there is virtually no engagement with themes of the new heaven and the new earth. It is not clear that the analogy of God as the "master chess player" can give both freedom to the other person involved in the game and bring the victory of good over evil. Has the insight into openness got to be held in a Wesleyan creative tension with the Creator God's assurance of new creation?

Wood has suggested that in the past divine providence has been allocated the time "in between" the world's creation and its consummation and has been drained of any creative significance.[93] Therefore, the emphasis in the doctrine has been on preservation, stability, order, and harmony, and the virtues it inculcates are mainly passive. He then argues that we must recapture the unity of creation and providence in order to see the "creative character" of the doctrine. Yet he could go further to link this to new creation. In the Didsbury Lectures in 1990, Colin Gunton suggested that creation is *to an end*, which is that all that is within space-time be perfected in praise of the creator.[94] Moltmann views Christian eschatology not as ending but as beginning with new creation, when creation is finally taken up into life of Trinity.[95] To recapture the unity of creation, new creation and providence strengthens all, giving providence in particular both an encouraging and challenging voice into Christian lifestyle.

93. Wood, "How Does God Act?"
94. Gunton, *Christ and Creation*.
95. Moltmann, *Coming of God*.

Advocates of openness see their position as a motivation to Christian responsibility and action, as our free human agency can make a difference.[96] Certainly, the sense of human freedom and therefore agency is significant, but Wesley's understanding of new creation gives confidence alongside this opportunity. God's plan for new creation demonstrated in the death and resurrection of Jesus is about the eventual triumph of good over evil. We can believe that we can make a difference but also that the end is assured. This gives confidence to Christians alongside opportunity. This is essential to the "optimism of grace."

New creation is based in the evidence of the death and resurrection of Jesus. Indeed, that resurrection is the exemplar or first fruits of that which is to come. We saw in Wiles the attempt to resist any sense of bodily resurrection from the fear of an interventionist God and the subsequent problem of evil. But Wesleyan theology has, with much other contemporary theology, reaffirmed the importance of Trinitarian theology.[97] It is this that gives another key orientating perspective on the doctrine of providence. Again, Wood rightly pointed out that in systematic theology providence has been seen in relation to the Father with the neglect of any christological or pneumatological considerations.[98] Thus, the tendency is to see the providential God as the Supreme Being of philosophical theism, with God's actions being determined by natural theology. Such a sterile doctrine of providence is corrected by Trinitarian thinking. God is both transcendent and immanent, acting as Creator and Sustainer, incarnate in Christ, who dies on the cross, and manifest in the power and presence of the Holy Spirit, pervading the church and the world. This reminds us once again that the nature of God's providential action is complex and how we perceive it is also complex. The triune pattern is the way God relates to all things but is also the pattern of our knowledge of that relation. To the extent that we can understand how God is related to what goes on, we understand it "through Jesus Christ" and "in the Holy Spirit."

Trinitarian thinking has often been neglected in the area of providence in favor of logic or science. It safeguards a specifically Christian understanding while posing creative questions to the doctrine. An example

---

96. For example, Boyd, *God of the Possible*.

97. Gunton, *Promise of Trinitarian Theology*; Wainwright, *Doxology*; Greggs, "On the Nature, Task and Method of Theology"; Greggs, *Dogmatic Ecclesiology*; Cho, "Wesleyan Trinitarian Theology and Pneumatology."

98. Wood, "How Does God Act?"

of this can be found in Pannenberg's attempt to describe the work of the Spirit in terms of the force of a field, as an immaterial force causes physical changes.[99] Much can be said against such a suggestion, but it does raise the question about whether some generalized physical theory can serve as meaningful metaphor for God's cosmic presence and, indeed, about the limits of such a metaphor.[100] We will return to the importance of Trinitarian thinking in the next two lectures.

Finally, a Wesleyan perspective will bring to the discussion of providence *the importance of prevenient grace*. Here is Wesley's understanding of God's free and generous acting in the world, which both gives responsibility to his creatures and characterizes his own responsibility as creator and redeemer.[101] God's purposes are achieved in relationships of response and responsibility. In terms of personal salvation, God is active before conversion, during conversion, and in the growth to holiness. God is active in both preparing this path and in active help along the way. Therefore, in terms of models of providence, Maddox is right to comment:

> While the longstanding Wesleyan commitment to God's responseability resonates strongly with the process emphasis on God's temporal, creative, and persuasive nature, it should be no surprise that this same commitment renders many Wesleyans less happy with the apparent restriction of God's role in the ongoing process of the whole of reality to only that of "lure." Is such a God still truly response-able? Where is the basis for eschatological hope within this restriction? Is there not a place for God to engage us more actively than this, without resorting to coercion?[102]

Wesley's understanding of grace reminds us of God's free, continuous, and multi-faceted activity. Further, it is a reminder that we cannot save ourselves. Whatever freedom is given to this creation, we cannot reach our potential in isolation. However we want to speak of the doctrine of sin, our freedom is severely limited by our rebellion against the God whose intimate relationship with us makes us fully human. Helm makes the forceful point that, "Our plight is such that only a God who can effectively bring

---

99. Pannenberg, "Theological Appropriation of Scientific Understandings."

100. See, e.g., Wicken, "Theology and Science."

101. Maddox, *Responsible Grace*; Cobb, *Grace and Responsibility*; Langford et al., *Grace upon Grace*; Crofford, *Streams of Mercy*; Shelton, *Prevenient Grace*.

102. Maddox, "Seeking a Response-Able God," 142.

about his redemptive aims . . . can help us."[103] Outler argues that grace is "the mainspring of any proper Christian doctrine of providence."[104] Due to grace, God is truly free to allow evil and yet sovereign to veto its final triumph.

In the light of this Wesleyan perspective, we will want to move away from models that are simplistic, models that do not do justice to the breadth of God's purposes or nature, and models that rob God or ourselves of real freedom and responsibility in the universe. All of the models have their limitations, but they also have value. As David Bartholomew wisely comments, "It is more important to establish that God could act in a world of chance than to discover how he does it."[105]

---

103. Helm, "Openness Theology," 50.
104. Outler, *Who Trusts in God*, 123.
105. Bartholomew, *God of Chance*, 143.

3

The Messiness of Miracle

Exploring Scripture and Experience

3.1 From Marge Simpson to Flying Bibles

WE HAVE SO FAR surveyed scientific and theological models of providence. Within popular culture and within most ordinary theology at the level of congregations, providence is often reduced to miracle.[1]

In a classic episode of *The Simpsons,* a hurricane hits the town of Springfield.[2] Cowering in their basement, Marge prays, "Dear God, this is Marge Simpson. If you stop this hurricane and save our family, we will be forever grateful and recommend you to all our friends." The hurricane disappears leading Homer to the theological comment, "He fell for it," and Marge to say it will all work out if you have faith. Most of the town is unscathed. However, the only house completely destroyed is that of their devout Christian neighbor, Ned Flanders. Taking shelter in the church whose noticeboard reads, "God welcomes his victims," Ned experiences a crisis of faith. Asking the pastor, Rev. Lovejoy, whether this is God's punishment, the response he gets is, "Short answer, yes, with an if; long answer, no, with a but."

---

1. Astley, *Ordinary Theology*; Astley et al., *God in Action*; Astley and Francis, *Exploring Ordinary Theology.*

2. www.imdb.com/title/tt0701131.

How Does God Act in the World?

It is a very clever comedic piece illustrating the way religion shapes the US context.[3] But it also illustrates the problems of miracles and prayer. Why does God work in some ways in answer to prayer but not in others? Ned is not the only one to experience a crisis of faith when God seems to be silent in the face of illness and suffering while fellow Christians testify to God working, often in trivial ways.[4] How important is faith and, more fundamentally, can God interact with the physical world at all?

If this is a picture embedded in Western popular culture, let me give you a very different picture from a different context. I was attending a seminar on evangelism in the UK, when one of the speakers, a Methodist minister from a country in Africa, told the following story. He was asked by his President of Conference to go a village of an unreached people. It was reported that previous missionaries had been attacked. He went with an interpreter, and after a few days preaching the gospel in the village, one of the elders told him that he needed to leave as he was attacking their gods of nature. Threats were made. The minister said he would leave the following morning. During the night, while they slept, someone crept into their hut and stole his Bible and Methodist hymn book. In the morning, he went to the elder and said that he was not leaving without his Bible and Methodist hymn book. (Incidentally, not the first Methodist to risk death by clinging on to the Methodist hymn book!) He and his interpreter stood in the middle of the village and prayed. He felt the Lord say, "Go to the river." They went to the river by the edge of the village and prayed again. As they prayed, his Bible and hymn book rose out of the river and landed on the bank in front of them. The speaker then paused in the telling of this story and looked around at the seminar audience, who were mainly white Western males. He then said, "I know what you are all thinking at this point. You have all been educated in a context shaped by the philosophy of David Hume. Your questions at the moment are all about the law of gravity and how can books defy it. You are also asking about the reliability of witnesses in such primitive societies. These are all fair questions, but in that moment in the village the primary question was different—that question was: Who was the most powerful, the Lord Jesus or the gods of nature?" I found this a profound moment when I realized that the questions of Western philosophy are not normative, especially for the global church.

---

3. Pinsky, *Gospel According to the Simpsons*.
4. Greig, *God on Mute*.

The Messiness of Miracle

In a major, two-volume work on miracles, New Testament and Pentecostal scholar Craig Keener has explored the subject from the perspectives of the biblical material and philosophy while helpfully bringing into the conversation accounts of the miraculous from different global and historical contexts. The number of claims of the miraculous is astonishing across different theological traditions and churches, across different religions, across all cultures, and throughout history. He argues that "anti-supernaturalism has reigned as an inflexible Western academic premise."[5] In contrast, he suggests that in response to miracle claims from eye witnesses, which are often neglected by biblical scholars, supernatural explanations should be welcomed on the scholarly table along with other explanations. As a New Testament scholar, he reports how his Western materialist assumptions about reality alienated him from the world of the book of Acts.[6] In addition, as he saw within the context of own his church community what he believed were divine healings, he began to question these materialist assumptions. Now there is an important point in his argument that claims of the miraculous do not constitute proof, but they do constitute evidence that may be considered rather than dismissed a priori.

Here we are back with Walter Wink: "People with an attenuated sense of what is possible will bring that conviction to the Bible and diminish it by the poverty of their own experience."[7] In these lectures so far, we have argued that certain pictures of science have attenuated our sense of what is possible. But they are pictures of science that give us a very limited view of the universe or have been misused philosophically to restrict thinking about God's action in the world. The commonsense everyday experience of the world has been understood through the lens of the Newtonian mechanistic universe and then projected onto what God can or cannot do. After two lectures on the science and theological models of God's action, in this lecture we will engage with the biblical material more directly. But we need to recognize two things that Keener has highlighted. First, the way that the Newtonian model has been brought as an interpretative framework to the miracle stories of the New Testament. We saw it in Bultmann, but he is not alone. Gerd Lüdemann in writing on the Acts of the Apostles commented,

---

5. Keener, *Miracles*, 2. See also Keener, *Miracles Today*; Kee, *Christian Origins in Sociological Perspective*, 3–12; Sabourin, *Divine Miracles Discussed and Defended*, 14; Eddy and Boyd, *Jesus Legend*, 372–73; Saler, "Supernatural as a Western Category."

6. Keener, *Acts*.

7. Wink, "Write What You See," 6.

"one ought not to begin with the assumption that miracles occur."[8] Talbert is right in responding, "The materialistic worldview, represented by Lüdemann, dictates that the world was and is ruled by iron physical laws that not even God could or can bend."[9] Pope Benedict XVI also pointed out that dismissal of the miraculous was not primarily due to biblical scholarship but to philosophy.[10] We have already argued that the world of twenty-first-century science is more supple and subtle and does not impose these "iron physical laws."

Second, the Newtonian worldview fed into the development of the philosophy of David Hume, and his argument against the miraculous became one of the strongest influences on thinking about how God acts in the world. So, in this lecture we will need to engage with the legacy of Hume.

We will then move on to focus in on the question of miracles, both in terms of how they are viewed in the Bible and how they can be viewed in the light of science today.[11] I will suggest that the experience of miracles is messy in the biblical material, but they are also messy in that they disrupt our attenuated sense of what is possible. What will need to wait until the next lecture is a discussion of the problem of evil, which as we have seen is one of the major problems for any view of God that gives God the freedom to do particular and unusual acts in the world.

3.1 Hume, Miracles, and Biblical Interpretation

The Scottish philosopher David Hume (1711–1776) is a central figure in the discussion of miracles. There have been a number of critiques of his argument, but he remains influential both in the academic and popular arenas.[12] His own religious views are difficult to fully untangle. Some of his contemporaries regarded him as an atheist but was this because they did not fully understand Hume's arguments. In addition, in a time of religious persecution by both church and state, we must ask whether Hume hid his

---

8. Lüdemann, *Acts of the Apostles*, 23.
9. Talbert, *Reading Luke-Acts in Its Mediterranean Milieu*, 215.
10. Jaki, *Miracles and Physics*.
11. Brown, *Miracles and the Critical Mind*; *That You May Believe*.
12. Earman, *Hume's Abject Failure*; Johnson, *Hume, Holism, and Miracles*; Houston, *Reported Miracles*; McGrew and Larmer, "Miracles."

real views.[13] Whatever the case, what is clear is that Hume was a skeptic who questioned any knowledge claims held as belief or dogma.[14]

To understand Hume's questioning it is important to understand the context in which he posed his challenges, in particular the kind of belief about miracles that was common in his day. Peter Harrison has helpfully set out this context in the histories of early modern science and religion up to the seventeenth century.[15] First, in the early modern period, Harrison suggests we witness a clear shift in the religious function of miracles. That is, they are seen less from the context of faith and become more a central element in the rational justification of religious beliefs. So, for Aquinas, miracles were not proof of the Christian faith but "confirmation." Hume inherits this context where miracles are used as an apologetic argument for the non-believer. Second, this shift in the understanding of miracles reinforces a new conception of religion as having less to do with inner virtue, specific ritual practices, or being part of the body of Christ and more to do with intellectual agreement to a set of rationally justifiable propositions. This has been a very important insight from Harrison not just for this period but for the overall dialogue of science and theology.[16] Therefore, in this shift, religious truth could now be expressed in propositional terms that could be tested in spheres beyond the authoritative structures of the church. In a time when new expressions of Christian faith were emerging in the light of the Protestant Reformation these tests became more and more important. Mainstream Protestants were especially committed to this, aiming to expose the falsity of claims of Roman Catholicism or new enthusiastic Protestant churches. Third, natural philosophy came to play this important role in the adjudication of rival religious claims, especially when it came to miracles. Natural philosophers studied the ordinary course of nature, which was important if miracles were an exception to that normal course. In addition, their work gave them experience in judging the reliability of testimony. Harrison comments that the combination of these shifts was that the discussion increasingly was less about *which* miracles were true and more about whether *any* miracle, in principle, could happen.

---

13. Russell and Kraal, "Hume on Religion"; Graham, *Great Infidel*.

14. Laursen and Paganini, *Skepticism and Political Thought*; Danford, *David Hume*; Norton and Taylor, *Cambridge Companion to Hume*; Parusnikova, *David Hume, Sceptic*; Pupo, *David Hume*; Smith and Garrett, *Philosophy of David Hume*.

15. Harrison, "Miracles, Early Modern Science."

16. Harrison, *Territories of Science and Religion*.

How Does God Act in the World?

Hume needs to be understood against this background. He is responding to those Christian apologists who were using miracles to prove God and the Christian understanding of God.[17] This included some eminent names such as John Locke (1632–1704), Robert Boyle (1627–1691), and Samuel Clarke (1675–1729), who commented: "The Christian Revelation is positively and directly proved, to be actually and immediately sent to us from God, by the many infallible Signs and Miracles, which the Author of it worked publickly as evidence of his Divine Commission."[18]

Gaskin has suggested that Hume in his essay "Of Miracles" was responding to this approach and in particular to Thomas Sherlock's *Tryal of the Witnesses of the Resurrection* (1729), which ran to seventeen editions.[19]

While Boyle and others saw no problem in using natural philosophy to ask questions both of contemporary experience and of the biblical stories, the shifts that Harrison outlines moved the discussion of miracles away from biblical theology to the realm of philosophy. As we shall see later, the messiness of the biblical narratives was therefore smoothed over to more general philosophical considerations. This is where Hume becomes extremely important.

His discussion "Of Miracles" occurs as the tenth section of his *An Enquiry Concerning Human Understanding* (1748). This section was sometimes omitted, with Hume worried that it might cause too much offense to religious people.[20] At one level, offense could be taken by those who saw it as a direct attack on core doctrines such as the resurrection:

> When anyone tells me that he saw a dead man restored to life, I immediately consider with myself, whether it be more probable, that this person should either deceive or be deceived, or that the fact, which he relates, should really have happened.... If the falsehood of his testimony would be more miraculous, than the event which he relates; then, and not till then, can he pretend to command my belief or opinion.[21]

But more of a challenge was a collection of arguments that would form the core of a critique of miracles for centuries to come. Of the many arguments, let me pick out four that are key for our discussion in these lectures.

17. Burns, *Great Debate on Miracles*, 57–69.
18. Clarke, *Evidences of Natural and Revealed Religion*, 695.
19. Gaskin, *Hume's Philosophy of Religion*, 149.
20. This has been published separately as Hume, *Of Miracles*.
21. Hume, *Enquiry Concerning Human Understanding*, 89.

The Messiness of Miracle

First, Hume argued that historical research depends on analogy. To evaluate the plausibility of accounts in the past they have to be compared to events that we experience in the present. Here Keener and others are right to point out that our own limited experience can constrict the analogies with which we work. Hume had limited knowledge of the science of his day—that is, the Newtonian worldview—and a limited bank of experience, especially in global terms. Therefore, to judge the plausibility of the accounts of the New Testament by our own limited experience is something we need to be very careful about.

Second, Hume regarded miracles as violations or contraventions of natural law. In this he was followed by others, including Voltaire.[22] Indeed, this has been Hume's lasting legacy, with a definition of miracle as a contravention of the scientific laws. Yet this definition is dependent on a number of scientific and theological assumptions.

In terms of science, this view sees the natural laws as deterministic, prescriptive, and complete. Historians of science generally accept the contribution of the Judeo-Christian worldview to the forming of the concept of the laws of nature. As God is the faithful, universal, and communicative creator and sustainer of the whole of the universe, there should be regular patterns that are consistent throughout the universe and could be understood by humans made in God's image.[23]

But we often confuse the ontological status of these laws in both academic and popular discussions. As we have seen in lecture 1, the laws do not necessarily imply determinism. Indeed, the physics of the twentieth century in terms of quantum theory and chaos have shown exactly the opposite. You can understand the laws but cannot predict the future. Further, the "laws," as we call them, are always provisional. Our formulations of them change as science progresses, giving us not a full, complete description but models that exhibit verisimilitude to reality. All models are limited by the data they are based on and sometimes by the mathematical framework which they are dependent on. Therefore, the laws of science should be seen more as descriptive rather than prescriptive.

---

22. Besterman, *Voltaire*; Johnson, *Voltaire's Contribution*.

23. Zilsel, "Genesis of the Concept of Physical Law," 245–79; Needham, *Science Religion and Reality*; Oakley, "Christian Theology and the Newtonian Science"; Foster, "Christian Doctrine of Creation"; Padgett, "Roots of the Western Concept."

Imagine for a moment we see the following graph of two variables, x and y, with a number of points, some of which have error bars attached to them indicating the uncertainty in measurement.

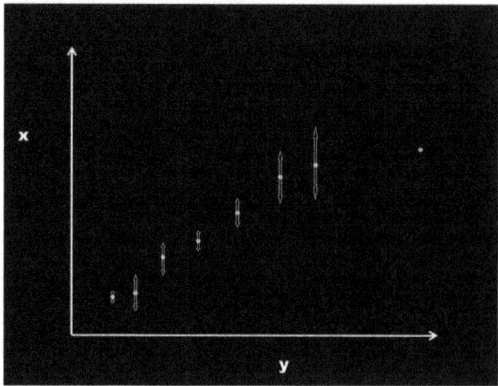

The majority of points suggest that the relationship of x and y can be represented by a simple straight line.

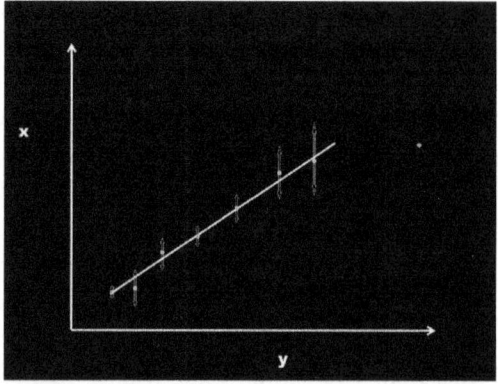

But what about the outlying point on the far right? Does it fall onto the straight line of the others, or does it represent a new phenomenon? It could be an errant measurement, and if an error bar was added to it, then the line might be extended through it. But if this experiment is about the heating of a beaker of water at sea level, where x represents the temperature of the water against y the length of time of heating, we understand this graph in a different way.

The Messiness of Miracle

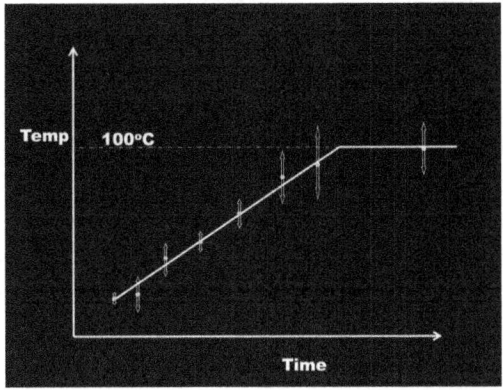

When the water boils the temperature will remain the same. This phase change is not predicted by the regular relationship of temperature and time up to this point of 100 degrees centigrade.

So, the laws of physics describe our observation of patterns in the universe, they do not necessarily rule out unusual phenomenon, which may be the result of other, deeper laws or may not be encompassed by the particular laws that we observe.

The theological assumptions of Hume's contravention of the laws of nature are equally fragile. The laws of nature can be viewed as completely autonomous of God. Or for Spinoza (1632–1677), in pantheism, God was identified directly with the natural order. Therefore, for God to create the natural laws and then suspend or contravene them would be God going against God. But the Christian doctrine of *creatio ex nihilo* does suggest that the whole universe and the laws that sustain it are created from nothing by God. The laws are therefore a reflection of God's sustaining action, God's normal patterns of working.

Harrison highlights that such a view was held in part by Newton and his contemporaries, such as Robert Boyle. He suggests that they had "a dual commitment to the mechanical universe . . . and an omnipotent God who intervened in the natural order from time to time breaching these 'laws' of nature."[24] Some historians have put this down to naïve thinking which ignored the ambiguities and inconsistencies inherent in such a position. Rather, Harrison argues, Newton and others rejected the definition of miracle as violation of laws of nature. For example, Samuel Clarke, the greatest advocate for Newton, argued against natural laws being seen apart

---

24. Harrison, "Newtonian Science, Miracles," 531.

from God and thought that miracles are the unusual actions of God. They thus denied that any philosophical sense could be made of the claim that miracles were breaches of natural law. Harrison also refers to an unpublished manuscript by Newton on the apocalypse, commenting that "the possibilities of nature for Newton were nothing less than the possibilities of the omnipotent Deity."[25] This is particularly interesting, and we will return to it later in the lecture.

The distinction, then, between natural and supernatural was not part of the tradition leading up to Hume. Hume introduces the concept of miracle as breaking the laws of nature, which were seen as complete, prescriptive, and deterministic.

Third, Hume argues that there is a problem of eye-witness accounts of miracle. Yet his argument has more than a touch of circularity to it.[26] Based on the assumption that miracles do not happen, he then dismisses eyewitness testimony to the miraculous. For Hume, no testimony is sufficient to establish a miracle as it is outweighed by the uniform experience of modern people against miracles. Further, only credible witnesses should be believed, and such credible witnesses have to be reliable, highly reputable, religious observers, who will only be that if they know that miracles are irrational.

Fourth, Hume contends that different religions claim miracles and thus their claims cancel each other out. Here Hume is reflecting the way that religious believers were attacking each other in the area of miracles.

You will gather that I do not find Hume's arguments compelling! Yet his influence on biblical interpretation and thinking about God's action in the world, coupled with the Newtonian mechanistic worldview, has been profound in several ways. Ruling out a priori God's direct activity in particular and unusual events in the natural world led to a number of responses of biblical scholars.

Jean Jacques Rousseau (1712–1778) saw God working at the level of the universal, not the particular. God does not interfere with his own laws of nature. Rousseau therefore suggested that miracles might be explained naturally and only appeared miraculous to those who did not know better.[27] This followed a tradition of seeing natural explanations of biblical

---

25. Harrison, "Newtonian Science, Miracles," 533. See also Manuel, *Religion of Isaac Newton*, 101.

26. Campbell, *Dissertation on Miracles*, 31–32.

27. Oelkers, *Jean-Jacques Rousseau*; Rousseau, *Letter to Beaumont*.

miracles. The deist John Toland (1670–1722) had suggested naturalistic explanations for Old Testament accounts such as the pillar of cloud and fire.[28] Heinrich Paulus (1761–1851) likewise suggested natural explanations for biblical events.[29] The disciples were confused by the circumstances and misreported them. So, for example, Paulus argued that Jesus walking on the water was in fact him walking by the shore rather than on the sea, and that the disciples in the middle of night thought they were in the middle of the sea when in fact they had been blown towards the shore.[30] Similarly the feeding of the five thousand was not a miraculous production of bread and fishes but rather the example of the small boy sharing his contribution shamed the whole crowd into sharing their own packed lunches. This approach is patronizing in the extreme. It ascribes to the disciples and the authors of the Gospels both gullibility and lack of knowledge. It is difficult to believe that fishermen who had spent their lives on the Sea of Galilee would make such a mistake. Paulus was among a number of scholars who extended this approach to the so-called "swoon theory," which claims that Jesus did not die but passed out on the cross and came back to consciousness in the cool of the tomb.[31] There was no resurrection as there was no death. This idea featured in the thought of Oscar Wilde and resurfaced in a number of popular books.[32]

If Paulus's approach was about misunderstanding, there were others, such as Hermann Samuel Reimarus (1694–1768), who claimed that the miracles were about deception. He was a deist and dismissive of revelation. He is seen by some as the one of the first scholars to investigate questions around the historicity of the Gospels, giving birth to the quest for the historical Jesus.[33] His *On the Intention of Jesus* (1778) was published anonymously and posthumously. Reimarus argued that the disciples had created a different religion to what Jesus had intended. Jesus had intended a political kingdom of God, expelling the Romans from Jerusalem. He had miscalculated his popularity and was subsequently executed. The disciples, facing the reality of this failure, created the resurrection account by stealing the body from the tomb, thus creating a new religious movement of which

---

28. Toland, *Tetradymus*; *Christianity Not Mysterious*; Herrick, "Miracles and Method."
29. Paulus, *Das Leben Jesu*; Ehrman, "Jesus, Apocalyptic Prophet," 25–26.
30. Chisholm, "Paulus, Heinrich Eberhard Gottlob."
31. Stevens, *Historical Jesus and the Literary Imagination*.
32. For example, Baigent et al., *Holy Blood, Holy Grail*.
33. Klein, *Hermann Samuel Reimarus*; Schweitzer, *Quest of the Historical Jesus*.

they would be leaders. In the words of Marcus Borg, for Reimarus, "Christianity was the invention of their conniving minds."[34]

A different option for responding to the difficulties posed by Newton and Hume came in David Friedrich Strauss's *The Life of Jesus Critically Examined* in 1832. In it, Strauss (1808-1874) argued the miracles were myths created by the early church to express theological truth about Jesus. He took seriously that the Gospels do present miracle accounts as miracles, rejecting the approach of Paulus. He also rejected Reimarus's approach of deception. Yet he finds it impossible to imagine a physical intervention of God. Instead, the Gospel writers use images from the Old Testament coupled with religious imagination to fashion stories that communicate the significance of Jesus.

Strauss is not arguing that the miracle stories are created to deceive, but that they are true in a different way: "The supernatural birth of Christ, his miracles, his resurrection and ascension, remain eternal truths, whatever doubts may be cast on their reality as historical facts."[35]

This approach had a lasting impact on Western scholarship.[36] But it is predicated on Newton and Hume and a view of the universe that, as we have seen, is now outdated. Thus, reviewing the resurrection, Strauss comments that God's particular action in this is "irreconcilable with enlightened ideas of the relation of God to the world."[37] This is a consistent theme for his judgment of all miracles, "indeed no just notion of the true nature of history is possible without a perception of the inviolability of the chain of finite causes, and of the impossibility of miracles."[38]

Alongside, this misuse of science and philosophy came another, more subtle impact for biblical scholarship. The definition of miracle as a contravention of the laws of nature is often assumed to represent and have represented the Christian understanding of miraculous phenomena.[39] Peter Harrison rightly suggests that by putting the discussion of miracles first through the filter of philosophical theology and then bringing it back to biblical scholarship, the rich diversity of the biblical material and Christian

---

34. Borg, "Search Begins."

35. Strauss, *Life of Jesus Critically Examined*, 5.

36. Beiser, *David Friedrich Strauß*; Twelftree, *Jesus the Miracle Worker*, 32-33; Theissen and Merz, *Historical Jesus*.

37. Strauss, *Life of Jesus Critically Examined*, 736.

38. Strauss, *Life of Jesus Critically Examined*, 75.

39. Burns, *Great Debate on Miracles*; Earman, *Hume's Abject Failure*.

tradition is negated.[40] He points to this diversity in the way the biblical authors describe such events as "signs," "wonders," "mighty works," and, on occasion, simply "works."[41] The absence of a distinct terminology reinforces the important observation that the authors were not working with the Humean sense of a "contravention of the laws of nature" which has become so standard for modern readers. It also leads us back to a recognition of the messiness of miracles.

3.2 Encouraging Humility and Hope in What Is Possible

Even if these lectures were a yearlong weekly series rather than the current four, the discussion so far will indicate the impossibility of being able to give a definite account and model of how God works in what is commonly spoken of as "miracle." However, noting that theology often acts as an activity that cautions you what *not* to say rather than an easy articulation of the nature of God, let me offer four suggestions that I find helpful in thinking about the miraculous as a scientist and a theologian. For me, they encourage a perspective of humility and hope in what is possible.

3.2.1 Surprising Science

Polkinghorne's discussion of the cloudiness of the worlds of quantum theory and chaos, and the subsequent lessons for thinking about the physical world led him to point to the danger of being dominated by common sense. The world of the everyday is for most people a world that is predictable and picturable. But alongside this we have also seen that the "laws" of science are limited and provisional. While they do give us a tightening grasp of reality, they are not the whole story.

The history of science illustrates this very well. The Newtonian description of the universe, so influential for Hume and for subsequent generations of theologians, reigned supreme up to the beginning of the twentieth century. Indeed, by that point physics had described the orbit of the planets and in Maxwell's theoretical formulation of the equations of electromagnetism had explained the nature of light in a way that new

---

40. Harrison, "Miracles, Early Modern Science."

41. Kittel et al., *Theological Dictionary of the New Testament*, 2:284–317; 7:200–261; 8:113–26.

technologies were springing up from it. Physics was near retirement; its work had been done. However, there were one or two minor unresolved issues, including what medium light as a wave travelled through (the ether) and the fact that the orbit of Mercury did not quite fit with what was expected.

In a revolutionary use of the scientific imagination, Albert Einstein solved these minor problems and opened up a view of the universe that was light years away from common sense. He suggested that the speed of light was the same however you measured it, and this led to theories of Special and General Relativity.[42] The implications were profound. The measurement of time depended on motion so that, contrary to our everyday expectation, clocks run slow if you accelerate them close to the speed of light, while mass increases and length contracts. Further, the mass and distribution of matter determines the geometry of space and the rate of flow of time. This became the foundation for the major development of cosmology as well as essential to enabling Sat Navs to get us to the right location![43]

Relativity did not throw out the Newtonian descriptions of motion. At low velocities and away from strong gravitational fields, the equations of Newton work well. Indeed, the equations of relativity reduce to Newton in these circumstances. But relativity shows us that Newton is only a very small description of reality. In a similar way to quantum theory and chaos, there is a reality that is far more surprising than our everyday experience would expect. This is part of the gift of science. T. F. Torrance commented on the basis of relativity that because we cannot perceive the structure of space-time by our senses, it encourages a humility towards surprising aspects of our experience of the universe as a whole.[44] That is not to say that miracles are all due to "deeper laws" that we have not yet discovered, but it does give an openness to new possibilities beyond our current understanding of the laws of physics.

Such humility is also important in helping us to not think of the laws of science as prescriptive in a theological sense. To rule out a particular action of God because it "contravenes" the natural laws is a misunderstanding of the nature of scientific models and a misunderstanding that the laws are a description of God's normal ways of working. Humility recognizes that

---

42. Einstein, "Zur Elektrodynamik Bewegter Korper," 891; "Grundlage der Allgemeinen Relativitätstheorie," 771.

43. Kaku, *Physics of the Impossible*.

44. Torrance, *Space, Time and Incarnation*.

God as creator and sustainer of the laws may exercise freedom to transcend God's normal ways of working to do particular and unusual acts in the universe.

It is here that some theologians are way behind some of my scientific colleagues. The provisional nature of science is also a caution to locking God's action too closely with the scientific description of the world. Polkinghorne's location of God's activity in the hiddenness of chaotic systems is insightful, but it may not be the whole story. It may be susceptible to a god-of-the-gaps critique. Furthermore, as we shall see, the hiddenness of divine action does not fully represent the New Testament material, which speaks not merely of God's hiddenness but also of miracles as a sign of exactly the opposite.

3.2.2 Surprising Experience of the Global Church

Keener's summary suggests that belief in miracle is widespread, across the global church and among those who are not part of Christian communities. Even in the post-Christian West this is the case, with 60 to 80 percent in the US claiming to believe in miracles and 34 percent of people claiming to have experienced divine healing.[45] In his *Miracles Today: The Supernatural Work of God in the Modern World*, Keener interviews a number of people who have claimed healings and also doctors who have been involved. He also provides hundreds of eyewitness accounts from around the world, from the healing of cancer to resuscitation of the dead.

Keener is not without critics. In particular, Peter May, a retired GP and fellow Christian, has worked for decades investigating modern miracles stories and remains unconvinced by the evidence.[46] His critique of Keener at times is a little unfair, but he makes an important point about the value of rigorous skepticism as an essential ingredient in the search for truth.[47] This is different from the cynic who manipulates the evidence for confirmation of their own view. Further, May points out the difficulty of assuming that the miracles of Christ are no different from the healings that are claimed today. Some use this assumption to argue that Christ performed miracles because such things are so often witnessed today. But there are considerable

---

45. Keener, *Miracles Today*, 204.
46. May, "Miracles Today?"
47. May, "Claimed Contemporary Miracles," 144–58.

differences; for example, the Gospel accounts show Jesus healing at the word of his command.

Some Christians have argued that God's action in the miraculous is no longer part of the experience of the Christian church. At the time of the Protestant Reformation, as we have seen, miracle claims were used by both Roman Catholic groups and Protestant offshoots to claim their authenticity as the church of Jesus. To counter such claims, mainstream Protestants, such as John Calvin, began to insist that the age of miracles had ceased. They had occurred during the time of Jesus and the apostles to confirm the truth of the gospel but now were not needed. Indeed, Calvin went further to warn against false prophets performing signs and leading people astray. This became a strong approach in Reformed theology.[48]

Yet the growth of Pentecostalism and the charismatic movement worldwide has given a renewed emphasis on signs and wonders as manifestations of the kingdom. From the origins of the Pentecostal revival in Azusa Street through to the ministry of John Wimber and beyond, the experience of spiritual gifts and healings have been part of the story.[49] Indeed, there would be those who would argue that it was because of the manifestations of signs and wonders that the mission of these movements has been so successful.[50] Yet such signs and wonders have been claimed throughout Christian history.[51]

It seems to me that we need to be open to such claims and yet at the same time follow the biblical encouragement to test the spirits. May is right to want to pose serious questions to those who claim the miraculous, not least because we know that many have used such claims to manipulate people for their own financial gain or oppressive power. Humility and hope encourage both the scientist and the theologian to examine carefully each account of signs and wonders, open to the work of the Holy Spirit moving

---

48. Warfield, *Counterfeit Miracles*.

49. Blumhofer, *Restoring the Faith*; Robeck, *Azusa Street Mission and Revival*; Burgess and Maas, *New International Dictionary*; Anderson and Hollenweger, *Pentecostals After a Century*; O'Connor, *Perspectives on Charismatic Renewal*.

50. Alexander, *Signs & Wonders*; Wimber and Springer, *Power Evangelism*.

51. Ward, *Signs and Wonders*; Korte, *Women and Miracle Stories*; Koopmans, *Wonderful to Relate*; Cooper and Gregory, *Signs, Wonders, Miracles*; Thomas, *Religion and the Decline of Magic*; Yarrow, *Saints and Their Communities*; Bartlett, *Miracles of Saint Aebba*; Crisafulli et al., *Miracles of St. Artemios*; Finucane, *Miracles and Pilgrims*; Gardner, "Miracles of Healing"; Goodich, *Miracles and Wonders*; McCready, *Miracles and the Venerable Bede*; Rieder, *Miracles and Heretics*; Shaw, *Miracles in Enlightenment England*.

in unusual ways. Moving the language from "miraculous healing" to "signs and wonders" may be helpful. Keener sees such events as "extraordinary signs... special acts of God that get attention and communicate something about him" and as "a divine action that transcends the ordinary course of nature and so generates awe."[52]

The wealth of material of these claims often defies any system of categorization. Perhaps that is simply part of the territory of a personal God who acts in particular and surprising ways.

3.2.3 Surprising Biblical Witness: John 2

Most New Testament scholars will accept that the Gospels present Jesus as a miracle worker and that he believed himself to be a miracle worker.[53] But this is not unique in ancient literature, where there are numerous miracle claims outside of Christianity. Belief in and reports of widespread miracles exist in Greco-Roman and Jewish worlds, associated often with shrines and charismatic individuals.[54]

Yet there is a messiness to the New Testament accounts and their interpretation.[55] As we have already noted, they are mainly classed as signs and wonders, but what they are signs *of* can vary, from the kingdom of God to the identity of Jesus, from the compassion of God to the power of God.

As an illustration, let us take a moment to look at Jesus at the wedding in Cana (John 2:1–11). While most standard commentaries note the centrality of questions of Christology and eschatological promise using the imagery of water into wine, few have noted the surprising aspects of this narrative.[56]

The first is the *surprising location* in the flow of John's Gospel. The Gospel has begun with the cosmic significance of Jesus. The prologue has located the story of Jesus in the heart of creation and how God's Word had

---

52. Keener, *Miracles Today*, 3.

53. Rowland, *Christian Origins*, 146–47; Dunn, *Jesus Remembered*, 671.

54. Strelan, *Strange Acts*; Theissen and Riches, *Miracle Stories*; Cotter, *Miracles in Greco-Roman Antiquity*.

55. Busse et al., *Miracles and Imagery in Luke and John*; Latourelle and O'Connell, *Miracles of Jesus*; Moule, *Miracles*; Warrington, *Miracles in the Gospels*; Wenham and Blomberg, *Miracles of Jesus*.

56. Morris, *Gospel According to John*; Barrett, *Gospel According to St John*; Brown, *Gospel According to John*; Sloyan, *John*; Carson, *Gospel According to John*; Beasley Murray, *John*.

become flesh (John 1:14). Jesus is then identified as the Lamb of God who takes away the sin of the world (1:29), the Son of God (1:34), the Messiah (1:41), and the King of Israel (1:49). And then "on the third day" (2:1) sets up for the Christian reader a suggestion of the resurrection triumph of Jesus. The scene is set, and in the light of the end of chapter 1 finishing with, "You shall see greater things than that. . . . I tell you the truth, you shall see heaven open and the angels of God ascending and descending on the Son of Man" (1:51), the reader might be expecting some kind of blockbuster confrontation with the political and religious authorities or a dramatic sign. Clearing the temple courts might be such a dramatic sign, but that has to wait until after this sign performed at a wedding in Cana (2:13–25).

This leads us, second, to a *surprising setting*. The "first of the signs through which he revealed his glory" (2:11) was performed at Cana in Galilee. Now the imagery of a wedding feast between God and Israel would be powerful but a wedding in Cana in Galilee is surprising. This was not a "wedding of the year" in Jerusalem with the nation's leaders in attendance. This was a sign not at a religious shrine but a wedding of two unnamed people in a place, Cana, that was so unremarkable that scholars do not definitively know where it was. John gives us a sense that Jesus was not there as a key guest, as he says that Mary was there, and Jesus and his disciples had also been invited! I have been to a number of weddings where I "had also been invited," where I do not know terribly well the member of the family or friend of my wife. This possibly awkward situation was compounded with the socially embarrassing situation of running out of wine. This was the setting in which Jesus first "revealed his glory" in a sign.

As David Day in a talk once characterized it: Imagine an unnamed couple, perhaps Tracey and Darren, who in ten years' time when they show the video of their wedding to their friends, say, "Oh yes, here's the buffet, here's my mum with that fascinator, here's Uncle Albert being sick on the dance floor, bless him, and by the way, here's when the Son of God first revealed his glory."

C. K. Barrett points out a parallel to the god Dionysus, who was not only the discoverer of the vine but also the cause of miraculous transformation of water into wine. But the setting was worship in temples, not a wedding in Cana.[57]

---

57. Barrett, *Gospel According to St John*, 157.

The Messiness of Miracle

Third, this is a *surprising sign*. Indeed, its nature was even called by Hengel "profane."[58] The turning of between 120 to 180 gallons of water into wine at a wedding feast when most of the guests have already drunk a lot seems both extravagant and odd. Grayston, who has a high degree of skepticism over historicity, nevertheless raises the question of whether the water was actually turned into wine.[59] He suggests two possibilities: either the guests were given appropriate mental stimulus to perceive water as wine or the water underwent atomic transformation from a compound of hydrogen and oxygen to a compound of carbon, hydrogen, and oxygen.

This could be in a fundamental changing of the substance of matter, or it could be the way that we perceive matter. What is interesting is that the Gospel is presenting in the sign a very clear demonstration (whether historical or in story) of the capacity that God possesses for the transformation of matter.

The fact that the stone jars were filled with water for ritual washing (v. 6) is of course significant. Did the water represent the old order that Jesus was to replace with something better? The interpretation is not absolutely clear. This story has in some ways the nature of a parable, which draws the reader in to ask deeper questions without a clear definitive interpretation. In fact, for John, the signs do point to a deeper reality, which in the structure of the Gospel are often linked with the "I am sayings" and festivals. Yet this sign does not seem to fit that pattern as much as other signs. Nevertheless, this sign points to *who Jesus is* and the response is that "the disciples believed in him" (v. 11).

What however strikes me (as a teetotal Methodist!) is what appears to be the excess of the sign. This is a picture of Jesus far removed from monastic asceticism of hermetic communities. Wedding celebrations could last as long as a week, and the financial responsibility lay with the groom. Running out of wine resonated with a shame culture and aggrieved relatives of the bride. Is the excessive provision of so much wine pointing to the extravagant generosity of God or the lavish provision of the new age? Yet I don't think it is unreasonable to ask, why not a clearer sign?

Fourth, we might also note the *surprising exchange* between Jesus and his mother. His mother notes "they have no more wine" (v. 3). This is not only an observation but also a request. I know a similar thing when my wife says to me, "The bins have not been put out!" Somewhat oddly, Jesus

---

58. Hengel, "Interpretation of the Wine Miracle."
59. Grayston, *Gospel of John*.

replies, "Woman, why do you involve me? . . . My hour has not yet come" (v. 4). It is difficult not to read this as mild rebuke, and yet Jesus goes on to answer the request in the most extravagant way.

Put all of these things together and you might think that if this is the Gospel writer creating a myth about who Jesus is, then he could have done a better job. A miracle that was a clearer sign, done at a significant place with significant people, would have been a much better story. Yet this is about God at work in the ordinary with ordinary people in an account that does not quite fit nor is easy to interpret. For me, the messiness of many of these signs not only has "the ring of truth"[60] but also is a reminder that simple understandings of how God may or may not act in the world need to be treated with great caution.

3.2.4 Surprising Bodily Resurrection

We noted in the previous lecture that Wiles's model of divine action, where God is the sustainer of the physical process but does not intervene in the physical world, struggled with the bodily resurrection of Jesus in such a picture. Wiles shows commendable honesty in noting this.

In his major work, *The Resurrection of the Son of God*, Tom Wright argues that the resurrection, denied by pagans but affirmed by many Jews, was both reaffirmed and redefined by the early Christians. The pagan world assumed it was impossible, the Jewish world believed it would happen eventually, but Christians said it had happened to Jesus. Further, in the early Christian community there was no spectrum of belief but an almost universal affirmation of resurrection, seen in terms of bodily resurrection. The future hope of Christians was based on their firm belief that Jesus had been raised from the dead. Wright sees this claim as open to historical study, which he carries out in some detail.

Wright has not been without criticism, not least in whether he can claim that there was no spectrum of belief regarding resurrection in the early Christian community.[61] Yet I find his approach convincing, not least in the surprise of the resurrection happening in Jesus and that this resurrection was bodily. Wright is strong on the need to avoid a loose usage of "resurrection." Sometimes, it is used of a disembodied "heavenly" life or

---

60. Phillips, *Ring of Truth*.

61. Carnley, *Resurrection in Retrospect*; Dunn, "Review"; Patterson, "N. T. Wright"; Powell, "Review."

continuation of the soul,[62] or even, according to some scholars, of a person's inner "religious experience" of Christ's "risen" life.[63] Others have argued that the sense of Jesus being raised on the third day is that he was exalted into heaven.[64] Indeed, it is claimed that the resurrection narratives grew up following a belief in Jesus' exaltation, producing "apologetic legends" of an empty tomb, "bodily" stories of the risen Jesus to combat Docetism, and a second-stage ascension.[65]

However, the surprising nature of the resurrection narratives do not quite fit these positions. There is a surprising lack of reference to Old Testament imagery and indeed a lack of application to personal hope in the resurrection narratives, which might be expected if the stories had been created for theological reasons.[66] Further, if the Gospel writers were to invent the stories, we might have expected that their risen Jesus would be the vision of a dazzling figure of Jewish apocalyptic tradition (Dan 12:2–3) or that the first witnesses would not be women (for women were often considered unreliable witnesses). On both counts we would be surprised.[67] Finally, if the stories had been created, then we would expect them to be much tidier and consistent than they are.[68]

As Williams says of the resurrection narratives:

> They do not fall tidily into familiar genres; they do not easily present themselves as fulfilments of prior expectation. . . . They are painfully untidy stories, reflecting sometimes all too plainly the various political interests at work in the formulation of the tradition, yet containing more than those interests can manage. The central image of the gospel narratives is not any one apparition but the image of an absence, an image of the failure of images, which is also an absence that confirms the reality of a creative liberty, an agency not sealed and closed, but still obstinately engaged with a material environment and an historical process.[69]

---

62. Davies, *Death, Burial and Rebirth*; Porter, "Resurrection, the Greeks," 68.

63. Schillebeeckx, *Jesus*; Goulder, "Baseless Fabric of a Vision," 48.

64. Evans, *Resurrection and the New Testament*, 83; Perkins, *Resurrection*, 28–29; Carnley, *Structure of Resurrection Belief*, 18; Harvey, "They Discussed," 74.

65. Bultmann, *History of the Synoptic Tradition*; Robinson, "Jesus from Easter to Valentinus," 5–37; Riley, *Resurrection Reconsidered*.

66. Williams, *On Christian Theology*, 195.

67. Bauckham, *Gospel Women*, 268–77.

68. Wedderburn, *Beyond Resurrection*.

69. Williams, "Between the Cherubim," 100.

Part of this messiness of the resurrection accounts is not only the divergences between the Gospel accounts reflecting different sources and purposes but also the clear indication that the Jesus who died is both the same and different to the Jesus who was raised.

The Gospel narratives emphasize the physicality of Jesus, showing the wounds of the cross and eating with the disciples.[70] Yet there is more than just physicality. These things have often been so overemphasized that expressions of Christian belief in popular piety and apologetics have bordered on physical resuscitation rather than resurrection. But Christ's resurrection is not similar to Lazarus. Although the disciples know that this is the same Jesus, he seems to have different physical characteristics. They have trouble recognizing Jesus both in the garden and on the road to Emmaus, and some continue to doubt (John 20:14; 21:4, 12; Matt 28:17; Luke 24:37). Further, Jesus did not seem to be limited to space and time, appearing in rooms with locked doors (John 20:19–20), and there is a real sense of mystery to the resurrection appearances (Mark 16:1–8).

The account of the disciples on the road to Emmaus gives an interesting example of how exegesis has been dominated by continuity more than discontinuity. The two disciples walk miles with Jesus without seeming to recognize him (Luke 24:13–35). Commentators give many suggestions as to why, including that the Sun was in their eyes, their eyes were filled with tears, or that they were too frightened to look around! Others more convincingly see the revelation of Jesus in the Scriptures and in the breaking of bread being key to the passage.[71] However, the obvious point is that Luke is telling us that Jesus was somehow different. Jesus in some way has transcended the constraints of his earthly life. He is the Jesus that the disciples knew, but he is different.[72] I have suggested elsewhere that this is a transformation to a more than physical existence where the relationship with matter, space, and time is changed.[73] It is this discontinuity of the transformation of the body and how to represent this discontinuity that adds to the "untidiness" of the Gospel accounts.

There has of course been a strong strand to Pauline scholarship which has argued that Paul knew nothing or thought little of an empty tomb. This is centred on 1 Corinthians 15. What is immediately striking in the short

---

70. Gundry, "Essential Physicality of Jesus' Resurrection."
71. Crüsemann, "Scripture and Resurrection."
72. Marshall, *Gospel of Luke*, 892–900.
73. Wilkinson, *Christian Eschatology*.

summary of the gospel (vv. 1–11) is there is no reference to the empty tomb. This has been used to argue that the empty tomb was not important to the early Christian preaching or was consciously ignored to promote the authority of the male disciples over the women who were first at the tomb.[74] Marxsen and others have suggested that Paul's description here could be simply interpreted in existentialist terms.[75] John Barclay cautions against narrowing our options at this point, due to the breadth of meaning in the noun "resurrection" (*anastasis*) and in the verb "to raise" (*egeiren*) and the jumble of views about the afterlife held by first-century Jews.[76] However, the juxtaposition of "he was buried" and "he was raised" surely implies an empty tomb, especially in the context of first-century Judaism, where resurrection would predominately be thought about in physical terms.[77] This cannot therefore be interpreted simply as "Christian experience."[78] Paul sees the resurrection as a public event with witnesses of a specified number and an implied empty tomb.

The empty tomb is a clear indication of the resurrection of the body of Jesus, demonstrating the transformation rather than the discarding of the body. The implication of this is that if the resurrection of Jesus is the "first fruits" of God's purposes for all creation (1 Cor 15:20–28) then it is the model for the relationship of old and new creation, and that God's purposes for the material world are that it should be transformed, not discarded. Bodily resurrection challenges the disconnect between the resurrection of Jesus and the future of the physical universe.[79] As Polkinghorne commented, "I believe that a downplaying of the empty tomb and of bodily resurrection, is a severe impoverishment of our eschatological understanding."[80]

We do need to be careful here. The analogy between the resurrection of Jesus and the resurrection of our own bodies in new creation resurrection

---

74. Ruether, *Sexism and God Talk*, 10–11; Borg, "Irrelevancy of the Empty Tomb."

75. Marxsen, *Resurrection of Jesus of Nazareth*; Patterson, *God of Jesus*.

76. Barclay, "Resurrection," 18.

77. Sider, "St Paul's Understanding"; Fee, *First Epistle to the Corinthians*, 725; Pannenberg, *Systematic Theology*, 358–60; Hays, *First Corinthians*, 256; Ware, "Resurrection of Jesus"; Cook, "Resurrection in Paganism"; Elledge, *Resurrection of the Dead*; Finney, *Resurrection, Hell, and the Afterlife*; Blanco, *Why Resurrection?*

78. Thiselton, *First Epistle to the Corinthians*, 1197–202; N. T. Wright, *Resurrection of the Son of God*, 318.

79. Peters, "Resurrection"; Russell, "Bodily Resurrection," 4; "Eschatology and Physical Cosmology," 295; Wilkinson, *Christian Eschatology*.

80. Polkinghorne, "Eschatological Credibility," 49.

cannot be extended too far. There is a short timescale between Jesus' death and resurrection, with his physical body preserved from decay, while in our case the timescale is extended, and our physical body will have decayed. The resurrection of Jesus occurred in history, exalts him to his rightful place as God's Son, and has universal redemptive significance. This is quite different to the general resurrection, which will occur at the eschaton. In this sense we need to remember that the first fruits indicate the harvest is coming but are different from the harvest in certain respects. While the empty tomb stands within the space-time history of this creation, the resurrection body of Jesus is better suited to the fullness of new creation. Indeed, it is only until the discontinuity of God's action in the parousia to transform fully this creation that Jesus in resurrected bodily form can return. The empty tomb is the demonstration of God's purposes in transforming creation, while the ascension and parousia speak of the limits of the current phase of creation's story.

These are not easy questions. The biblical literature here is complex.[81] However, the bodily resurrection of Jesus is a surprising, provocative challenge to those who follow Greek dualism and see God as only interested in the spiritual and those who do not see God as having the capacity to interact with the physical creation.

O'Donovan suggests that the resurrection is God's vindication of creation and our created life. Using the parallel between Christ and Adam, he argues that the resurrection is the affirmation of the initial gift of life and a transformation of that gift of life (1 Cor 15:22, 45):

> It might have been possible . . . before Christ rose from the dead, for someone to wonder whether creation was a lost cause. If the creature consistently acted to uncreate itself, and with itself to uncreate the rest of creation, did this not mean that God's handiwork was flawed beyond hope of repair? . . . Before God raised Jesus from the dead, the hope that we call "gnostic," the hope for redemption from creation rather than for the redemption of creation, might have appeared to be the only hope.[82]

But further, bodily resurrection says that creation can be transformed. It is not bound to its own inherent potential. Kennedy commented that the only "organic" link between this body and the glory to come is "the sovereign

---

81. Brannon, *Hope of Life after Death*; Chase, *Resurrection Hope*; Harris, *Refiguring Resurrection*.

82. O'Donovan, "Political Thought of the Book of Revelation," 90.

power of God."[83] The key to resurrection and new creation is not the importance of the material but the action of the creator God. The crucial point is that all things in creation and new creation are dependent on the creator's power. It is gift.

Thus, bodily resurrection first points us towards the importance of the action of God as a basis for hope for the future. The resurrection of Jesus questions a view of the world as a closed system with no room for God's action. The resurrection becomes a reminder of the importance of the action of God not just at the beginning of creation but at every moment and towards new creation.

Second, bodily resurrection points us towards the transformation of matter. The empty tomb demonstrates that the physicality of this world does matter to God and will not be completely destroyed or discarded. In terms of the future of the universe we expect God's actions to involve transformation of the physical universe rather than annihilation and beginning again. The biblical passages do not see new creation as God's "second attempt." Polkinghorne summarizes:

> The new creation is not a second attempt by God at what he had first tried to do in the old Creation. It is a different kind of divine action altogether, and the difference may be summarized by saying that the first creation was ex nihilo while the new creation will be ex vetere. In other words, the old creation is God's bringing into being a universe which is free to exist "on its own," in the ontological space made available by the divine kenotic act of allowing the existence of something wholly other; the new creation is the divine redemption of the old.[84]

So bodily resurrection is important because it is both about God's commitment to and interaction with the physical—both in terms of the universe and our bodies.[85] It provides historical evidence that can be examined, not to prove the nature and existence of God but to pose the question of whether God raising Jesus from the dead is the best explanation or model of this evidence.[86]

83. Kennedy, *St. Paul's Conceptions of the Last Things*, 243.

84. Polkinghorne, *Science and Christian Belief*, 167.

85. Allberry, *What God Has to Say*; Burreson and Hoeltke, *Death, Heaven, Resurrection*; Douglas, *Resurrection Hope*; Bieler and Schottroff, *Eucharist*; Hastings, *Resurrection of Jesus Christ*; Hickey, *Rising Light*.

86. Allison, *Resurrection of Jesus*; Habermas, *Risen Indeed*; Habermas et al., *Raised on the Third Day*; Dodson and Watson, *Raised?*; Habermas and Licona, *Case for the Resurrection of Jesus*.

How Does God Act in the World?

This leads back to our discussion of miracle. The bodily resurrection of Jesus is a surprising and shocking sign to a number of models of providence. It forms part of a number of aspects of Christian faith that do not reduce to simple models or may not be fully described by analogy or experience of this creation. Russell and Murphy wonder whether the resurrection of Jesus is the first instantiation of a new law of nature.[87]

We may conclude this lecture in which we have surveyed the miraculous by noting:

- Science does not constrain God from working in unusual ways.
- The laws of physics are a reflection of God's normal ways of working.
- We should approach unusual events with humility and curiosity.
- Miracles are not the way to prove the nature and existence of God.

In the next chapter our task will be to hold the nature of that faith in the context of mission and ministry and to put alongside resurrection the crucifixion of Jesus.

---

87. Murphy, "Resurrection Body and Personal Identity," 216–17; Russell, "Bodily Resurrection, Eschatology."

4

Witnessing to a God Who Acts

Implications for Mission and Ministry in the Contemporary Church

IN THESE LECTURES SO far, we have argued that contemporary science does not constrain theological thinking about God's action in the world in the way that many people, whether theologians or lay people, think it does. The Newtonian model is only a very small description of a much more subtle and supple reality. Models of how God acts in the world are shaped often by what they are reacting against, such as science or the problem of evil, and while giving some useful insights they do not do justice to the complexity of God's engagement with the world. In the last lecture we surveyed the philosophical background to modern discussion on miracles, which has shaped both the interpretation of the signs and wonders of the New Testament and the assessment of claims of the miraculous in the global church of today.

In this final lecture, my question will be how we bring the fruit of our discussion into the mission and ministry of the church, which often is tempted to one of two extremes—either a total absence of any expectation for particular divine action or expecting a miraculous answer to every prayer. Such expectations are not easy to live with. John Wimber's conversion to Christianity and his reading of the Bible led to his expectation that when he visited church for the first time he would see signs and wonders taking place as a normal part of ministry. He was somewhat disappointed! For most of the church in the West, there is little expectation that God is anything more than a spectator in the act of worship. If God does anything, then perhaps it is a warm feeling in the heart of the worshipper. As the Australian comedian Tim Minchin sometimes says, most Western Christians see God as a gentle hymn playing in the background.

At the other extreme, there are churches who give the impression that miracles can and should be part of the church's everyday life. In the 1992 movie *Leap of Faith*, Steve Martin plays Jonas Nightengale, a cynical preacher who uses revival meetings to con people out of their money. The movie lampoons the revival tent meetings of North America where evangelists wowed their audiences with supernatural healings. During one tent meeting, while the gospel choir sings, "Are you ready for a miracle?," Jonas feels a "healing coming on" and misleads the crowd with showmanship and the clever preparation of his team. The movie plays with issues of faith, disbelief, and evidence of healing, and the surprising event of an unplanned and unexpected miracle that shocks and changes Jonas.

Today you no longer have to have a tent ministry coming to your town, you can find all the claims you want on the web and indeed advice on how to pray for these miracles. Linda Evans Shepherd's *When You Need a Miracle: How to Ask God for the Impossible* claims to teach readers how to reach out to God and ask for a miracle. This book was endorsed by Don Piper, someone who claimed that he had spent, in the words of his book, *90 Minutes in Heaven*, having died for that period of time before being brought back to life. Piper says, "If you read this book until the end, you will experience miracles.... I read it. I did.... God makes the impossible possible every day. Sometimes we just need something to remind us how to ask for it."

Is there a way through this that keeps together cross and resurrection, the reality of evil and signs, uncertainty and witness? In the following I outline a number of anchor points that have been important in my own very limited experience as a scientist, church leader, and academic theologian, but most of all a disciple wanting to follow Jesus.

4.1 Taking Difficult Questions Seriously

Let us begin by looking at three pictures of science, the action of God, and the problem of evil to illustrate some of the power of these questions and to see different responses.

4.1.1 Two Scientists of the Nineteenth Century: A Biologist and an Astronomer

As he summed up his account *On the Origin of Species* (1859), Charles Darwin closed the last paragraph:

> There is grandeur in this view of life, with its several powers, having been originally breathed into a few forms or into one; and that, whilst this planet has gone cycling on according to the fixed law of gravity, from so simple a beginning endless forms most beautiful and most wonderful have been, and are being, evolved.[1]

However, in the second edition of the book (1860) he added the phrase "by the Creator" with the new reading: "There is grandeur in this view of life, with its several powers, having been originally breathed by the Creator."[2] But this inclusion of the creator was not to be maintained in later editions or in Darwin's view of life. In a letter to his friend Joseph Hooker, dated March 29, 1863, Darwin spoke of his regret that he had "truckled to public opinion & used Pentateuchal term of creation, by which I really meant 'appeared' by some wholly unknown process.—It is mere rubbish thinking, at present, of origin of life; one might as well think of origin of matter."[3]

His voyage on HMS Beagle (1831–1836) had shown him a grandeur in evolution revealed by the diversity of species on the Galapagos Islands but he had also seen another side. He had been shocked by a huge collection of fossils in a gravel bed in Argentina, and he had been literally shaken in the experience of an earthquake in Chile. These experiences showed him a world of competition, suffering, death, and unpredictability. This was a world very different to the world of intricate design by a creator God described by William Paley in his *Natural Theology* (1802), which had been part of Darwin's set reading as a student at Cambridge. Indeed, Paley had been a strong influence on Darwin's thinking and part of the reason why he joined the Beagle voyage:

> In order to pass the BA examination, it was also necessary to get up Paley's *Evidences of Christianity* and his *Moral Philosophy*. This was done in a thorough manner, and I am convinced that I could have written out the whole of the *Evidences* with perfect correctness, but not of course in the clear language of Paley. The logic of this book,

---

1. Darwin, *On the Origin of Species*, 490.
2. Browne, *Power of Place*, 95–96.
3. Darwin, "Letter to J. D. Hooker."

> and, as I may add, of his *Natural Theology*, gave me as much delight as did Euclid. The careful study of these works, without attempting to learn any part by rote, was the only part of the academical course which, as I then felt and as I still believe, was of the least use to me in the education of my mind. I did not at that time trouble myself about Paley's premises; and taking these on trust, I was charmed and convinced by the long line of argumentation.[4]

This charming, clock-like world was now crumbling for Darwin. However, worse was to come. His beloved daughter Annie became ill. Darwin prayed for her healing and took her to Malvern, where the waters were believed to have healing properties. Yet on April 23, 1851, shortly after her tenth birthday, Annie died. Nick Spencer has commented, "The last remnants of his belief in the good, personal, just, loving God of Christianity died at Easter 1851 with his dearly beloved daughter."[5]

Darwin's own personal beliefs remain somewhat mysterious. He was reticent to say too much, perhaps in part because of the strong Christian faith of his wife Emma. But Spencer is correct in identifying the turning point of the death of Annie and the problem that Darwin had in believing in a loving God who was able to interact with the physical world.

To another friend, Asa Gray, a Harvard paleontologist and evangelical Christian who had welcomed evolution, Darwin noted: "There seems to me too much misery in the world. I cannot persuade myself that a beneficent and omnipotent God would have designedly created the Ichneumonidae with the express intention of their feeding within the living bodies of caterpillars."[6] These wasps attack the immature stages of insects and spiders, eventually killing their hosts.

The problem of evil, the experience of unanswered prayer, and a view of a Paley's designer God all led Darwin to resonate with a number of thinkers that we have surveyed so far, commenting in his *Autobiography*, "The more we know of the fixed laws of nature, the more incredible do miracles become."[7]

Yet a contemporary of Darwin in the nineteenth century gives a contrasting story, even if there are many points of similarity.[8] Temple Chevallier

---

4. Darwin, *Charles Darwin*, 34–35.
5. Spencer, *Darwin & God*, 71.
6. Darwin, "Letter to Asa Gray."
7. Darwin, *Autobiography of Charles Darwin*, 86.
8. Wilkinson, "Proofs of the Divine Power?," 34–42.

(1794–1873) was a remarkable mathematician, astronomer, and theologian at the University of Durham. Chevallier entered Pembroke College, Cambridge, in 1813, taking a BA in 1817 with a strong mathematical flavor. In 1818 he was ordained in the Church of England and between 1821 and 1834 was priest at St. Andrew the Great in Cambridge. This must have been a formative period for Chevallier, as a scientist and a theologian, in a Cambridge as we have seen for Darwin heavily influenced by the work of William Paley. He accepted the chair of mathematics at Durham in 1835 and also became reader in Hebrew. In addition, in 1841 he became professor of astronomy and took the lead in establishing an observatory in Durham.

Chevallier cannot be understood without seeing him as a committed pastor as well as academic. Between 1835 and 1873 he served as parish priest of Esh. Yet the churchyard at Esh reveals common ground with the tombstone of Annie Darwin in a churchyard in Malvern. In Esh is buried Chevallier's only son, who died at the age of fifteen. This is always a reminder to me that people respond to tragedy in different ways. The death of his son was not the turning point for Chevallier in terms of faith that Annie's death had been for Darwin.

Chevallier's scientific work was not as significant as Darwin's, yet he made major contributions in astronomy and physics, including meteorology.[9] He was the first to institute in England regular and continuous observation of sunspots and made important observations of Jupiter's moons. So significant was his work that a lunar crater is named after him.

However, where he differs the most from Darwin is in his theological understanding, shown most clearly in his Hulsean Lectures given in Cambridge in 1826 and 1827, and then published in 1835, *On the Proofs of Divine Power and Wisdom Derived from the Study of Astronomy: And on the Evidence, Doctrines, and Precepts of Revealed Religion.*

The form of these lectures is instructive. They are given as twenty sermons on "the evidence for revealed religion." The first twelve lectures explicitly follow the pattern of Psalm 19, with four on astronomy, four on the Bible, and four on the spiritual life. These first twelve sermons show someone schooled in the Cambridge of Paley, yet holding together natural theology and the revealed theology of the Bible. While the "heavens proclaimed the glory of God," for Chevallier it was God's self-revelation in Scripture that convinced him of the existence and love of God.

---

9. Kenworthy, *Durham University Observatory*; Kenworthy and Lowes, "Chevalier Family."

From this perspective he saw science as a gift from God, rejoicing in insights from astronomy and mathematics. This engendered a sense of awe. Here the title of his lecture series is misleading in terms of "proofs." He is using science not as a logical knock-down proof of the existence of God but to give a sense of perspective, excitement, and amazement at the universe. It engages the emotions as well as reason. In popular descriptions of the design argument, it is often portrayed as an attempt to prove the existence of God. Chevallier has a much more modest aim in using awe to raise questions of how great God is. In this way, scientific laws are a reflection of God's working. He seemed to oppose any sense of what today is called a "god of the gaps,"[10] where God becomes the explanation for science's unanswered questions. Pointing to the laws of physics, as he does, is not appealing to a "god of the gaps," because those laws are assumed to exist by science. That is, science does not explain where the laws come from. That explanation is a *metaphysical* explanation. Any discussion of why there are any laws at all or why they are the way they are (as opposed to being different) would have to go beyond science. He does employ other pointers but not proofs of the design of the universe, including laws and circumstances that make life possible, including the distance of the Earth from the Sun, the stability of the planetary system, the seasons, the density of water, the density of the air, the proportion of land and sea, the tides, and the fact that Sun is the only luminous body in the solar system. It is very reminiscent of discussions of anthropic balances in recent years, but Chevallier never uses these circumstances to offer a proof for God's existence.[11] They are simply used as pointers to the creative skill of God in a universe that brings forth and sustains life.

For Chevallier, science has limits. God is known supremely because he reveals himself in Scripture, his word. As Chevallier works through Psalm 19, in lecture 5, he concludes: "But at this very point, where the feeble torch of reason ceases to direct our footsteps in the investigation of truth, the word of God shines forth, a lamp to our feet, and a light to our path."[12]

Biblical revelation gives the context to understand the pointers of awe, the laws, and design. Science has its limits in bringing us to knowledge of who God is. Indeed, in lecture 1 he had set the scene, criticizing those who

---

10. Coulson, *Science and Religion*, 7.
11. See Rees, *Just Six Numbers*; Davies, *Goldilocks Enigma*.
12. Chevallier, *On the Proofs of Divine Power*, 93.

have pride in reason and commenting (noting from above that Chevallier's use of "proofs" may be better understood as "pointers"):

> In the heavens, as in every other part of creation, there exist proofs of power and design. And if we stop short in our researches, without extending our thoughts from the wonders of nature to the God of nature, we omit to do that which reason recommends and revelation enjoins.[13]

It is Chevallier's commitment to holding together biblical revelation with his science that will, later in the century, allow him to respond to evolution without hostility or threat. Chevallier resonates with the argument of Livingstone that many of "Darwin's forgotten defenders" were those who had a strong commitment to the authority of Scripture.[14] This is where he departed from Darwin. Darwin's conception of a designer paid little attention to the concept of revelation in Scripture. There are strong arguments, contrary to the popular view, that negative responses to Darwin were not because it was an attack on Scripture but because it was an attack on the design argument.[15] This argument had become isolated from a commitment to biblical revelation. Thus, Darwin's alternative explanation for design attacked the core of the basis of belief in God. Chevallier did not share this approach and so did not feel threatened by Darwin.

The problem of evil affects different people in different ways. While Chevallier and Darwin no doubt experienced grief in different ways, perhaps part of the difference was that Chevallier held on to the love he saw primarily in Jesus.

4.1.2 Hymns About Earthquakes

On November 1, 1755, All Saints Day, Lisbon was hit by an earthquake and tsunami and then a subsequent fire which swept through the city. It killed between fifteen thousand and ninety thousand out of a population of two-hundred-and-seventy thousand. In this devout Roman Catholic city, the shock was not just the horrific death toll but that the disaster destroyed

---

13. Chevallier, *On the Proofs of Divine Power*, 9.
14. Livingstone, *Darwin's Forgotten Defenders*.
15. Wilkinson, "Work of a Friend."

most of the city's forty churches and ninety convents, while most of the brothels were left standing.[16]

The scale of this disaster for Lisbon led to a shaking of the foundations of Western thought.[17] For Kant and others, the science of seismology took on new significance. Philosophers began to use the language of "firm grounding" or "shaky arguments." Theologians had different reactions. Some were eager to point to God's judgment, from fellow Catholics, that the Lisbon churches were not good Catholics and from Protestants that the Lisbon churches were simply Catholic!

The more serious theological question underneath all of this was whether there a natural or a supernatural explanation. The assessment of Voltaire (1694–1778), published as "Poème sur le désastre de Lisbonne"[18] in 1756, was that this was not the best of all possible worlds and we live in a capricious and cruel world. This was a sustained attack on optimism and hope, reflecting on the fragility of life. In response, Rousseau attempted to defend providence and discussed human responsibility in the disaster.[19] For him it indicated the evils of progress and pointed to the need for human beings to return to a more natural way of life rather than inhabit cities. God was cruel or God was absent.

These were not the only responses to earthquakes. John Wesley, the founder of Methodism (with whom we have already engaged in these lectures), and his brother Charles were quite exercised by earthquakes and explored the theme in sermons, journal articles, and hymns. John Wesley's *Serious Thoughts Occasioned by the Late Earthquake at Lisbon* saw them in terms of God's judgment and even mentioned retribution for the sins of the Inquisition. The Wesleys had previously published *Hymns Occasioned by the Earthquake, March 8, 1750*, which referred to a series of earthquakes felt in London. These tremors in many ways had had a similar effect on English thinkers as the later Lisbon earthquake. There was much scientific speculation of whether they were purely natural phenomenon caused by subterranean air, water, or fire.

---

16. Mendes-Víctor, *1755 Lisbon Earthquake*.

17. Braun and Radner, *Lisbon Earthquake of 1755*; Brown, *Counterhuman Imaginary*; Hell and Schönle, *Ruins of Modernity*; Paice, *Wrath of God*; Shrady, *Last Day*.

18. Voltaire, "Poem on the Lisbon Earthquake."

19. Marques, "Paths of Providence," 33–57.

Yet for the Wesleys earthquakes were more than just accidents of nature, they were part of God's providential acts of punishment or protection.[20] They were part of the way that God both punished sin and gave warnings to people that they might awake, repent, and believe the gospel. The fragility of the world pointed people to the hope of salvation and trust in God.

Now it is not my view to follow Wesley on this. The use of natural disasters as God's judgment has been fraught with difficulties, from God causing the roof of York Minster to catch fire in 1984 to punish the unorthodox view of the newly ordained Bishop of Durham, Rt Revd David Jenkins, through to the flooding of New Orleans in 2005 due to its immorality.[21] The portrayal here is of a capricious God who does bizarre things often to bolster our theological prejudices.

However, I do suggest it is worth noting how the Wesleys saw this as an important subject for hymns and liturgy. Karen Westerfield Tucker sees this as part of a Christian tradition of supplementing authorized liturgical resources in times of national crisis.[22] It is the attempt to incorporate questions of the day into not only preaching but also into worship. The genre of hymns and liturgy allows a different type of exploration of the nature of God and the nature of humanity. The Wesley hymns go further, in pointing to a new creation. They herald that the "ruined world" is giving way to a "new created earth," the groaning of this creation, as Paul would describe it in Romans 8, which both laments the suffering of the present and points forward to the new birth of all creation. In this way there is an expression of earthquakes as the works of the Lord. Indeed, as Maddox has noted for John Wesley, if we set aside God's providential action in nature, we have no reason to hope for God's protection in any specific setting.[23]

In the struggle with evil, Christian liturgy has an important part to play. It holds the church from giving up on the belief that God is acting in all parts of the world. Through hymns, prayer, the reading of Scripture, and biblical preaching, it pays attention to themes of creation, incarnation, redemption, resurrection, judgment, and new creation.

---

20. Riss, *John Wesley's Reactions*; Fry, "Earthquakes and John Wesley," 98; Bassnett, "Faith, Doubt, Aid and Prayer."
21. Iyer, "Britain"; NBC News, "Hurricane Katrina."
22. Westerfield Tucker, "On the Occasion."
23. Maddox, "Hymn on the Lisbon Earthquake."

4.1.3 The Pandemic

A particular challenge for contemporary Christians has been the Covid pandemic, and how to speak about the action of God within this.[24] In the BBC podcast *Fortunately . . . with Fi and Jane* an episode during the pandemic saw Jane Garvey and Fi Glover talking with Australian comedian and composer Tim Minchin.[25] The conversation with Minchin, who is an articulate humanist, turned to questions of God during the pandemic, and Garvey raised her sense of surprise that church leaders had not been more public and vocal about it. Glover asked what Garvey wanted them to say and she responded, "Where is God in all of this?" At this point Minchin pointed out the excesses of what Christians have claimed in the past, affirmed the good that Christians were doing during the pandemic, and, as we noted earlier, said for most normal British Christians God is simply that gentle hymn in the background.

My immediate reaction while listening to this was a sense of anger. Many churches, including our own church in Jesmond, had gone to considerable sacrifice in making online worship and preaching available during times of lockdown. But although many services were publicly available on YouTube and Facebook, I began to see the force of the point that was being made. On the question of where God was in the pandemic, I and many others had been silent.

Shortly afterwards, our Equipping Christian Leadership in an Age of Science project hosted an online conference for senior church leaders on "Viral Science and Public Theology."[26] One speaker was a senior British politician who commended the work done by churches at the forefront of local communities in social caring, such as foodbanks. I saw the bishops and other senior church leaders almost swell with pride on their Zoom screens during this talk. But then the next talk was from a senior media news executive who said that he was disappointed by the lack of newsworthy stories from the churches during the pandemic. He wanted to have "heard more of a narrative" from church leaders on issues such as grief, compassion, and hope during a time when so many were wanting to hear about such things. At this point the polite faces on the screen became a little more twitchy. Subsequent

---

24. N. T. Wright, *God and the Pandemic*; Arbuckle, *Pandemic and the People of God*; Hampton, *Pandemic, Ecology and Theology*.

25. Garvey et al., "Conversational Sandwiches."

26. See www.eclasproject.com.

discussion exposed the perception that things were being talked about but also a reluctance to speak of some of the providential questions publicly.

My colleague at ECLAS, Dr. Thoko Kamwendo, followed this up with a series of in-depth interviews of twelve bishops of the Church of England during the pandemic. She showed that their theological understandings impacted their framings of the pandemic, not least leading to a reluctance to speak publicly about a theological interpretation of what was happening.[27] She found that the most consistently mentioned unhelpful narratives all hinged on an understanding of the pandemic as an act of God. She suggests that this was due to theological training resisting interventionist theologies, the fraught history of Christian commentators interpreting natural disasters as divine action, and wanting to maintain a focus on human agency and responsibility as the most appropriate response to the pandemic. However, there was one other reason. That was, to make space for the pandemic, the suffering and the virus that caused it had to be understood as part of creation.

So, our three pictures of the death of a family member, the shaking of foundations in earthquakes, and the challenge of a pandemic are reminders of the complexities of responding to questions of how God acts in the world. They are all about the reality of suffering and evil and a range of different responses. In the final part of this lecture series, I am not going to give an easy model for how God acts in the world. It will be patently clear from what we have explored above, and the brief sketch of previous Christian attempts to do this, that such an attempt is never going to be successful. That is not to say that some things cannot be said, even if they might be partial insights or fleeting glimpses of a reality much deeper. Rather, my concern is to ask, what are implications for the mission and ministry of the Christian church?

4.2 The Church Is a Community of Unanswered Questions and Pain

One option in response to how God acts in the world is to simply say that God cannot or does not want to act in particular ways beyond God's sustaining of the laws of physics. The position takes seriously the problem of evil but the God to be worshipped is not the God and Father of the Lord Jesus Christ and the giver of the Holy Spirit. Worship becomes an act of thanksgiving for God's creation and sustaining, but the sense of encountering a

27. Kamwendo, "Resistance to Narratives."

God who acts becomes non-existent. The preaching of the Bible becomes interpretation of symbol, of myth, and human encouragement to live a virtuous life. Prayers of intercession become affirming the need for human agency rather than expecting God to work alongside human agency in doing new things. The Eucharist is evacuated of much significance, for we lose the belief in a God who is present and a God whose eschatological fulfillment of the heavenly banquet is a promise, not a mere wish.[28]

Such a critique is unfair, but for those who believe that God does act in the world the difficulty in worship of their position also needs to be acknowledged. Believing that God answers prayer, acts in the world in particular events, and is working to bring about a new heaven and new earth in new creation in many ways makes the problem of evil worse. If God does certain things, why does God not do more and why does God do some things but not others?

This is where churches who believe in the miracle must also engage with the wealth and depth of the tradition of Christian worship. In particular, the expression of lament in worship is so important.[29] For the Anglican tradition, this is embodied in the regular rhythm of engaging with the Psalms, with all of their honesty of the problem of God not acting or God acting in unreasonable ways. There is grief, anger, longing for a better world, and the need to cultivate patience.

In the mid 1980s, I was student and was starting to preach and lead worship as a Methodist local preacher. Week by week we prayed for an end to the horrors of the violence and sectarianism in Northern Ireland. In 1983, the Irish rock band U2 released *Sunday Bloody Sunday* as a comment on those horrors, focused particularly on 1972's "Bloody Sunday," when British troops shot and killed unarmed civil rights protesters in Derry. The song is infused with Old and New Testament imagery, from the longing from Revelation of wiping tears away to the refrain of, "How long, how long must we sing this song?," resonating with the opening lines of Psalm 13:1–2. For someone longing for peace, such as myself, it became an important part of prayer, negotiating the complexity and expressing emotion.

Lament has to be part of a church where God is asked to act in particular ways. While testimony is often given by those who claim to have experienced the miraculous, there needs to be a place where unanswered

---

28. Wainwright, *Eucharist and Eschatology*.
29. Brown and Miller, *Lament*; Harasta and Brock, *Evoking Lament*.

prayers are acknowledged in the raw expression of anger and the development of patience.

Now it seems to me that lament presupposes a tension between revelation and mystery. It is precisely because the Psalmist believes that God can act that elicits both questions and trust. Trust in a God who has already acted in and is known in the exodus, but the God who declares, "For my thoughts are not your thoughts, neither are your ways my ways.... As the heavens are higher than the earth, so are my ways higher than your ways and my thoughts than your thoughts" (Isa 55:6–9). It is too simple an option to go to a God who becomes anthropomorphized and imaged in our experience of human everyday agency, but it is also too simple to retreat into stopping deeper questioning by saying "God moves in mysterious ways his wonders to perform."

Such a holding together revelation and mystery is helpfully explored by Boyer and Hall in *The Mystery of God*. To say that God is a mystery is not to confess our total ignorance; rather, it is to say that the mystery of God has been revealed in Jesus Christ. Here mystery and rational discussion based on God's self-revelation are not opposed but related. The mystery of God is a caution against the hope that rational discussion can understand all of God's ways of acting. Boyer and Hall suggest that, while we have good grounds for expecting that reason will be unable to master God the creator, we also have good grounds for believing that reason should not be abandoned as vain or worthless. They go on to note:

> But whatever approach one adopts, the reason Christians want to understand the mystery of God is not merely that they may set the metaphysical record straight, but that they may live and worship well—and life and worship depend on a right relation to a divine person more than on a right analysis of cosmic metaphysics.[30]

The revelation of the love and power of God, seen in Jesus, is a strong enough framework for holding the pain and anger of suffering when God is perceived not to act. That is why lament is so appropriate alongside the celebrating of the acts of God in praise and thanksgiving, in prayer for others, and in being sent out as servants and witnesses in the world. To engage with the question of how God acts in the world is not to find a perfect philosophical explanation but to be motivated and energized to pray and act.

---

30. Boyer and Hall, *Mystery of God*, xvii.

Here I might note that these lectures are being delivered in this distinguished theological college where the next generation of church leaders are being trained. The curriculum within British theological colleges and courses rightly holds together the theological exploration with the formation of the leader not only in pastoral ministry but also in a life of prayer and development of holiness. Part of that holiness is not a detachment from the pain of the world but an authenticity that embodies the grace of God within the pain of the world. For example, in the experience of the apostle Paul (2 Cor 12:7b–10), he speaks about his "thorn in the flesh." Some have argued that this is some kind of spiritual weakness, but I am persuaded by a number of commentators that it is most probably a physical affliction.[31] Paul intercedes for this to be removed on three occasions. But here his faith is expressed in his trust that God is at work even if his prayer for the thorn to be removed is not answered. It is particularly interesting that Paul is so open and honest about this, as the context of this letter of 2 Corinthians is that Paul is having to defend himself against criticism of his life and ministry, not least in contrast to those whom he calls the "super-apostles." Church leaders have a crucial role to be honest both to themselves and to the congregations that they serve. It is an easy temptation to look for, claim, and continually celebrate signs and wonders in order to validate one's ministry, indicating that we are "super-apostles," especially if financial support, career development, or self-worth needs to be delivered.

There is grace in seeing and living the brokenness and pain of the world alongside the proclaiming of a God who acts among us. One of the most poignant symbols for me of the pandemic came from the unveiling of the portrait of Professor Stuart Corbridge when he retired as vice chancellor of my own Durham University. The traditional portrait of a vice chancellor would be a commanding figure dressed in academic robes. When the portrait was unveiled it showed Stuart at home wearing a mask. He commented that he wanted this to demonstrate perhaps the most difficult role in his academic life, leading the University through the pandemic. I found it a most moving moment, and while Stuart would not identify as a Bible-believing Christian, I saw something of the Christian view of the authenticity of ministry in the portrait.

---

31. See Witherington, "Finding Paul's Weakness."

4.3 The Church Is a Community That Resists Unhelpful Narratives

It is clear from the discussion so far that I do think that the Covid pandemic is as important for my generation as the Lisbon earthquake was for a different generation. However, the immediate theological response in philosophy, theology, and hymnody has not had a parallel in the immediate aftermath of the pandemic. Indeed, discussion of the pandemic has been very muted. Perhaps the pain of it and the longing for life to return to normal has meant that we simply do not want to talk about it, rather like the experience of many soldiers after the trauma of war.[32]

Yet as we have seen, during the pandemic many Christian leaders wanted to distance themselves from certain theological narratives about the actions of God, in particular the punishment narrative. The Pew Research Centre suggested that 86 percent of US adults think the pandemic provided lessons for humanity, and 35 percent believed it to be a lesson "sent by God."[33] The real question however is, what *kind* of lesson? Was God punishing the evils of Western capitalism and immortality or was the lesson a more subtle one about how we have broken too often the sensitive relationship between human beings and the rest of the created world? When President Donald Trump stated that his own Covid illness was a "blessing from God," Christians rightly want to ask the question, what does that actually *mean*?[34]

One of my other colleagues in the ECLAS project, Dr. Franziska Kohlt, pointed out that both political leaders and some religious leaders in the UK framed the challenge during the pandemic in terms of conflict and war.[35] The then UK prime minister, Boris Johnson, adopted this rhetoric in order to rally public support in a national effort to "triumph" over the virus. This virus was evil, bent on destroying our way of life, and the discovery of a vaccine would enable us to "pummel it into submission." While it is understandable that such language should be used at a time of national crisis, it had huge and dangerous consequences. First, the "othering" of the virus saw it as a part of nature different from us. Second, a war framing allows a political structure to justify the experience of some as heroic. The

32. Putnam, "Hemingway on War and Its Aftermath."
33. Pew Research Center, "What Lessons?"
34. BBC, "Covid."
35. Kohlt, "Over by Christmas."

experience of NHS staff, ill-prepared and not provided with basic PPE, is to be applauded as heroic rather than something for which government has to take responsibility. Third, the use of fear to shape public thinking and action is immensely risky. In her book *A State of Fear,* Laura Dodsworth talks with people who were impacted by fear and isolation during the pandemic and suggests that at times fear was leveraged by those with power in the attempt to improve people's behavior.[36] But people respond to fear in lots of ways, sometimes with panic and sometimes by blaming others. Famously, in opening his inauguration speech at the peak of the Great Depression, Franklin D. Roosevelt asserted his "firm belief . . . that the only thing we have to fear is fear itself." Of course, Roosevelt went on to outline a plan for work and economic growth and a critique of selfishness in public life. It is interesting that he took his oath with his hand on the family Bible open to 1 Corinthians 13, a passage that talks about the priority and prevailing nature of faith, hope, and love.

Thoko Kamwendo has also commented on how the role of Christian leaders during the pandemic became that of Christian apologists for the decisions and public health directives of government. This is often the case in the time of national crisis, and here we may say that the backing of Christian leaders for lockdown, social distancing, and the importance of vaccination was important and wise.

However, the church is also the community that is a place of resistance to narratives that misrepresent the actions of God and in particular oversimplify models of God's relationship with human beings and the non-human creation. This is following the example of the Lord Jesus, who would take issue with current narratives with, "You have heard it said . . . but I say to you." The church always has to be a critical friend to government, culture, and its own institutional life. And at times, that friendship must be broken if it is simply being used.

So unhelpful narratives of God punishing in an arbitrary way have to be resisted as much as narratives that God only works "if you have enough faith." The Lord causes the Sun to shine and the rain to fall on both the righteous and the unrighteous (Matt 5:45). And the church needs to resist the narrative that human beings are masters of nature, subduing it and using it to their own ends. In 1967, the historian Lynn White argued that our ability to harness natural resources was marred by the deep-rooted assumption that

---

36. Dodsworth, *State of Fear.*

we are superior to nature, contemptuous of it, willing to use it for our slightest whim. . . . We shall continue to have a worsening ecological crisis until we reject the Christian axiom that nature has no reason for existence but to serve man. . . . Both our present science and our present technology are so tinctured with orthodox Christian arrogance towards nature that no solution for our ecological crisis can be expected from them alone.[37]

This "huge burden of guilt," in White's view, for the environmental crisis is in part a fair critique of an inadequate doctrine of creation held by many Christians. This inadequate doctrine of creation has been informed by a view of God that has often seen God acting only for certain human beings rather than as creator and sustainer of the whole physical and biological world.

In an interesting contrast to leaders adopting a warfare relationship with the Covid virus, two centuries earlier, Gloucestershire physician Edward Jenner published a pamphlet on his belief that vaccination could eradicate smallpox. During his apprenticeship as a surgeon, the teenage Jenner overheard a milkmaid repeat a popular belief she could not have smallpox because she had a cowpox sore on her hand from milking. Although such stories were dismissed as nonsense by many doctors, over the next thirty years Jenner studied the claim, and in 1796 he took material from a cowpox pustule on the hand of Sarah Nelmes and vaccinated eight-year-old James Phipps, who was rendered immune to smallpox. Jenner's paper detailing arguments and experiments however was rejected for publication by colleagues in the Royal Society, so he published it himself two years later as "Inquiry into the Cause and Effects of the Varioloe Vaccinae." After initial opposition, it became the foundation that would lead to a world free of the disease. It is interesting that Jenner did not speak of this as a battle or crusade against a malevolent natural enemy. He was passionate for truth and to relieve human suffering, and he also had a passionate love of nature, informed by his Christian faith, seeing it as God's creation. In an article in 1896, N. S. Davis drew attention to Jenner's "fondness for natural history," observing animal habits and also collecting fossils. This was a constant interest throughout his life. Sir Joseph Banks employed him to arrange the valuable specimens, zoological and otherwise, gathered by Captain Cook during his first voyage of discovery ending in 1771. Later in life, in 1823, Jenner presented a paper to the Royal Society on the migration

---

37. White, "Historical Roots," 1203.

of birds. Davis linked this love of nature to Jenner's "marked reverence for nature's great Architect."[38] In a letter to a friend written when he felt he had sufficient evidence for the genuineness of his discovery, Jenner says:

> While the vaccine discovery was progressive, the joy I felt at the prospect before me of being the instrument destined to take away from the world one of its greatest calamities, blended with the fond hope of enjoying independence and domestic peace and happiness, was often so excessive, that in pursuing my favourite subject among the meadows, I have sometimes found myself in a kind of revery. It is pleasant to me to recollect that these reflections always ended in devout acknowledgements to that Being from whom this and all other mercies flow.[39]

His respect for science and the natural world came from his sense of both being gifts from God. His faith also energized his practice of providing his vaccine for the poor in his own home.

To separate God's concern for the whole of the created order from God's concern for human beings is an unhelpful narrative. To separate God's particular acts in signs and wonders from God's sustaining of the laws of physics and our own free agency as human beings runs not only into theological error but, as a result, leads to the destruction and injustice of the climate catastrophe. To separate scientific exploration from claims of signs and wonders devalues the gift of God and the need to pursue truth.

Donald MacKay (1922–1987) was a British physicist and the founding professor of the Department of Communication and Neuroscience at Keele University. He is known for his pioneering contributions to information theory and the theory of brain organization. He often likened science to a child exploring his or her family garden, a place of wonders, mystery, and some dangers to be coped with. But this is a very different image to the triumph of a battlefield. In fact, for McKay, a Christian rather than pagan view of nature was a much more effective inducement to science:

> In place of the craven fear instilled by a pagan theology of nature—the fear of being regarded as an unwelcome and over-inquisitive intruder in matters that are not his business—the Christian who finds scientific talents in his tool bag has quite a different fear—the fear that his Father should judge him guilty of neglecting his

---

38. Davis, "Address."
39. Davis, "Address," 919.

stewardly responsibilities by failing to pursue the opportunities for good that may be opened up by the new developments.[40]

It is interesting that in all angelic visitations in Scripture the first words are "do not fear." This biblical refrain is based on a belief in a creator God who is active in the world and where the priority of love is focused on Jesus. Christian communities should be places where there is, in David Jenkins words, a sense of a transcendent God in the midst, but places where narratives of fear are resisted with stories of hope and humility.

In a study of public fears in the UK about the emerging field of nanotechnology, Phil Macnaghten and colleagues suggested that at the root of unease were strong narratives derived from Greek myths rather than the Judeo-Christian understanding.[41] Thus, "opening Pandora's box" or "messing in the realm of the gods" were strong themes rather than the positive theme of science as God's gift. The resistance of the church to these views of nature is just as important as resisting the corruption of the Judeo-Christian view into an arrogant use and abuse of creation.

Thus, within churches that have an openness to signs and wonders there needs to be an openness to becoming an ecochurch along with a commitment to science. It is to this that we turn next.

4.4 The Church Is a Community Where Science Engages Theology

Throughout these lectures I have tried to argue for an engagement with science as one discussion partner in the conversation about how God works in the world. Again, during the pandemic, politicians often used the phrase that their decisions were being "led by the science." The trouble with this claim is that science is not a monolith. It comprises a multitude of disciplines and approaches to the world which all have that quality of provisionality in their descriptions. This was illustrated time and time again. Epidemiologists disagreed on the strategies of whether or not to go into lockdown in dealing with a virus in the population. Advice on handwashing was slowly replaced with the importance of ventilation of spaces. And scientists working in mental health pointed out that while lockdown might limit the spread of the virus, it had other serious consequences for many people.

40. MacKay, *Open Mind*, 102.
41. Macnaghten, "Nanotechnology."

This dialogue, marked by disagreement between public health professionals and mathematical modelers, epidemiologists and psychologists, did not allow scientists or politicians to come to easy solutions. "Decisions are informed by science, they're not led by science," Sir Patrick Vallance told parliament's Health and Social Care Committee on April 5, 2020, in his role as the UK Government's chief scientific adviser.[42]

These insights are an important reminder of the nature of the dialogue of science with Scripture and theology. The engaging of science as a conversation partner is a multi-textured and open-ended enterprise where attention needs to be given to different scientific disciplines and the status of scientific models of the world. This requires theologians to be attentive and have a degree of scientific literacy within specific scientific disciplines. We have seen how theological models can be dominated by certain scientific understandings. The adoption of a clockwork, mechanistic view of the world stemming from Newton's laws of motion led to a number of theological claims that there was no room for God to work within the physical world in special providence or miracle, and this contributed to the demythologizing agenda within New Testament scholarship. Theology should not be "led by the science" in thinking about God's action in the world.

The provisionality and complexity of science means that theology needs to be *informed by* but not *dominated by* science. This works out in a number of ways.[43] First, science becomes one tool among many in hermeneutics, in interpreting Scripture.[44] John Polkinghorne has suggested that doing theology in a context of science has parallels in the approaches of feminist and liberation theologies.[45] This is helpful as long as we recognize the power dynamics involved. Feminist and liberation theologies come from those communities that have been disempowered. The difficulty of science is the power it wields in the modern world due its success. Indeed, the success and beautiful simplicity of the Newtonian worldview was part of its power in theology. But science needs to be brought into the web of interpretation of Scripture.

Second, the provisional nature of science means that its voice is to be heard with both humility and patience by the theologian. An interesting example of this can be seen in the latter part of the nineteenth century.

---

42. Tatalović, "Government Decisions."
43. Wilkinson, "Bible, Theology and Science."
44. Gilkey, "Cosmology, Ontology"; Moritz, "Hermeneutics of Science and Scripture."
45. Polkinghorne, *Theology in the Context of Science*.

In the midst of the cultural upheaval of the Darwinian controversies, over seven hundred scientists of the day signed "The Declaration of Students of the Natural and Physical Sciences" (1865):

> We, the undersigned Students of the Natural Sciences, desire to express our sincere regret, that researches into scientific truth are perverted by some in our own times into occasion for casting doubt upon the Truth and Authenticity of the Holy Scriptures. We conceive that it is impossible for the Word of God, as written in the book of nature, and God's Word written in Holy Scripture, to contradict one another, however much they may appear to differ. . . . We cannot but deplore that Natural Science should be looked upon with suspicion by many who do not make a study of it, merely on account of the unadvised manner in which some are placing it in opposition to Holy Writ. We believe that it is the duty of every Scientific Student to investigate nature simply for the purpose of elucidating truth, and that if he finds that some of his results appear to be in contradiction to the Written Word, or rather to his own *interpretations* of it, which may be erroneous, he should not presumptuously affirm that his own conclusions must be right, and the statements of Scripture wrong; rather, leave the two side by side till it shall please God to allow us to see the manner in which they may be reconciled.[46]

These scientists wanted to resist the tendency to denounce science for the sake of defending Scripture. Rather, they wanted to affirm science as a gift from God and to lay science and the Scriptures side by side, believing that the Author of both would not allow them to ultimately contradict. Patience and humility guard against the tendency to react by either attacking science or being dominated by a particular scientific model.

Third, as John Brooke has often noted, we need to avoid talking about a relationship of science and theology and appreciate a number of relationships, both in history and in the present, of particular scientific insights and projects and theological disciplines.[47] We should be careful therefore in our use of "science" as a unified voice. Here biblical studies can be in conversation with certain scientific insights even if there is no unified way of expressing the theology-science relationship. Polkinghorne thus spoke of "bottom-up" approaches being more fruitful than "top-down" approaches,

---

46. Brock and Macleod, "Scientists' Declaration," 41.
47. Brooke, *Science and Religion*.

emphasizing the importance of the particular issue in the dialogue of science and theology rather than becoming stuck in generalities.

I have attempted to do this in these lectures by taking specific scientific insights into the world and asking what questions they may pose for theology. Chaos and quantum theory may not give all of the answers on God's action for the world, but they do raise interesting challenges and new possibilities. I have also tried to take seriously the historical development of how science and theology have engaged, showing sometimes the limitations and new thinking that comes out of this. I have also tried to bring into conversation with the sciences both philosophical theology and biblical studies. Too often we have separated these things, not least within the theological academy. Part of theology's task is to inhabit the complexity and open-endedness of this conversation. In some ways this has similarities with the approach of Donald MacKinnon, the Norris-Hulse Professor of Divinity at Cambridge University, who in 1968 published *Borderlands of Theology and Other Essays*. MacKinnon was fascinated by how theology can join in conversation with arts and literature rather than existing in its own linguistic and cultural bubble. He also refused to simplify difficult questions in order to produce tidy or conclusive answers. His insistence on truth over tidiness is evident in his method of thought, an approach that some have labelled "open-textured."[48] The approach of MacKinnon is equally applicable to science as well as the arts. Indeed, it is embodied in Tom McLeish's understanding of the dialogue of theology, science, and the arts.[49]

I am conscious that there will be those among my readers who will want this methodology set out in far more detail. Practical theology has grown tremendously in recent years and there are a variety of models on offer.[50] (It is worth noting in passing that while these approaches in practical theology have engaged with the social sciences, there has been little engagement with physical and biological sciences.) Likewise, there have been countless typologies, from Barbour onwards, on how to relate science and theology.[51] All have a place. But I have approached these lectures with

---

48. Hardy, "Theology Through Philosophically Mediated Life."

49. McLeish, *Faith and Wisdom in Science*; *Poetry and Music of Science*.

50. Ballard and Pritchard, *Practical Theology in Action*; Cartledge, *Practical Theology*; Miller-McLemore, *Wiley-Blackwell Companion to Practical Theology*; Osmer, *Practical Theology*; Swinton and Mowat, *Practical Theology and Qualitative Research*; Browning, *Practical Theology*; Fowler et al., *Developing a Public Faith*; Root, *Christopraxis*; Ward, *Introducing Practical Theology*; Weyel et al., *International Handbook of Practical Theology*.

51. Barbour, *When Science Meets Religion*; Haught, *Science and Religion*; Peters,

a model of dialogue, where a conversation does not always have a strict agenda, rules, or agreed action points! The nature of conversation is at times spontaneous, fluid, or wandering away on tangents, with misunderstandings of language and argument which need to be returned to, but not necessarily within one solo conversation. The key to a good conversation is an openness to listen, to be honest, and to build communication and trust.

Looking for less complex alternatives can leave us with a deistic creator who sets the universe off and then retires from it or a divine being who is so constrained in the process of the universe that it is unable to do anything significant in the cosmos. Here the "messiness" of biblical theology subverts and critiques attempts to provide too simplistic and overly systematized accounts of God. What I mean by this is that the biblical writers in a wide variety of genres communicate a Trinitarian God who reveals but is at times mysterious, who is Lord of nature but vulnerable to death on a cross, and a Spirit who breaks down expectations and is as much at work in the world as in the church. As we noted in an earlier lecture, Wood rightly points out that in systematic theology providence has been seen in relation to the Father with the neglect of any christological or pneumatological considerations.[52] Thus, the tendency is to see the providential God as the Supreme Being of philosophical theism and his actions can be determined by natural theology. Such a sterile doctrine of providence is corrected by Trinitarian thinking. The nature of God's providential action is complex, and how we perceive it is also complex. The triune pattern is the way God relates to all things, but it is also the pattern of our knowledge of that relation. To the extent that we can understand how God is related to what goes on, we understand it "through Jesus Christ" and "in the Holy Spirit." Biblical scholarship in this area safeguards a specifically Christian understanding while posing creative questions about how we understand God's activity.

Within the worldwide growth of the Pentecostal church and the charismatic tradition in older denominations, the relationship between science, Bible, and signs and wonders is both a challenge and an opportunity. As we saw in lecture 3, the growing influence of this movement, with its belief in a God who acts in the present and in the local, is significant for Christian

---

"Theology and the Natural Science."

52. Wood, "How Does God Act?"

theology. Scholars within that tradition, such as Amos Yong, are key voices for the doctrine of providence to hear.[53]

Once again this leads us to ask, how might this play out in local congregations and the practice and training of church leadership? Am I arguing that a year-long lecture course in quantum theory and chaos should be a core module for every theological college and course? You will be relieved that I am not, even though I know that most of you would ignore me if I did! The theological curriculum is already overfull with limited time available for the training and formation of church leaders. However, there are a couple of things that could be done, which our ECLAS project has been exploring in recent years. "Science for Seminaries" was developed in the US, and rather than introduce new courses on science and theology into the curriculum, it took a different and more effective approach. This was to support theological teachers in introducing good science into already existing core modules within the curriculum. Thus, within systematics or biblical studies, can we help colleagues to engage with some contemporary science? Now some theologians already have a scientific background and interest and in this we need to give confidence to them that the insights of science are valuable within the core theological disciplines. But what about those colleagues who feel out of their depth with the science? Here there are many professional scientists, whether they are people of faith or not, who are enthusiastic about an invitation to come into a theological seminary to lecture or be interviewed about some of the scientific questions. In ECLAS we have so far successfully introduced "Science for Seminaries" into half of the UK theological colleges and courses.[54]

The same principle of recognizing the gifts of scientists in engaging with theology is also true in local congregations. Another one of our projects, "Scientists in Congregations," recognizes the vocations of those Christians who work as perhaps technologists, engineers, biology teachers, or even astrophysicists and asks how local church leaders can work together with them in the mission and ministry of the local church.[55] The result has been over sixty projects, which far surpassed our expectations. We initially thought we would simply get churches arranging lecture series on science and religion. But once you put scientists and church leaders into

---

53. Smith and Yong, *Science and the Spirit*; Yong, *Spirit of Creation*; *Spirit Renews the Face of the Earth*.

54. www.eclasproject.org/science-for-seminaries.

55. www.eclasproject.org/congregations.

partnership, the creativity is stunning. From books on Messy Science to projects of Take Your Vicar into the Lab, from dinosaur skeletons in cathedrals to plays about AI, churches have learned that in engaging science there is a source of untapped riches already within their congregation. The voice of professional scientists who are Christians in the area of how God acts in the world should not be underestimated. This is a question that all will have lived with in lots of different ways in their everyday working lives, not just in church on a Sunday.

In all of this, science is done by scientists. It is often more effective for non-scientists not to be taught science but to encounter scientists. This should not surprise a faith community that itself is based on incarnation.

4.5 The Church Is Community of Cross and Resurrection

In John 12, immediately after Jesus triumphal entry into Jerusalem, John describes how a group of Greeks approach Jesus. It is preceded by the Pharisees saying to each other, "See, this is getting us nowhere. Look how the whole world has gone after him!" (John 12:9). John picks this comment up with the Greeks, illustrating those beyond the Jewish people, seeing something in Jesus and contrasting those who are eager to encounter Jesus with the frustration of some of the religious leaders. While the Greeks had come to the religious festival, they could only be admitted to the Court of the Gentiles.

Why they wanted to see Jesus is not clear, but their request gives the Gospel a significant moment. While some scholars have tried to read significance into why they approached Philip first, there is no convincing argument.[56] Rather, for me, the comedic value to Philip having to consult Andrew and then, when they had enough courage, telling Jesus is far more compelling.

For Jesus, this enquiry is, as Carson notes, a "trigger ... that the climatic hour has dawned."[57] This "hour" is the hour of the glorification of Jesus, but of course in John it is a *single* movement of cross, resurrection, and exaltation. Indeed, the glory is fully displayed just as much in the brokenness of the cross as in the power of the resurrection. Jesus expresses this in an image from the experience of the natural world concerning a kernel of wheat:

---

56. Barrett, *Gospel According to St John*, 352.
57. Carson, *Gospel According to John*, 437.

> The hour has come for the Son of man to be glorified. Very truly I tell you the truth unless a kernel of wheat falls to the ground and dies, it produces many seeds. Anyone who loves their life will lose it while anyone who hates their life in this world will keep it for eternal life. (John 12:23–25)

While a number of commentators here focus on the death of Jesus generating a large harvest of those who can experience eternal life, there is another dimension to these words. The motif of the cyclicity of nature was represented in many other ancient religious beliefs as well as used by Jesus in Synoptic parables (Mark 4:3–9, 26–29, 30–32; Matt 13:3–9, 24–31; Luke 8:4–8; 13:18).[58] Donald English, several years ago, did not want to separate the saving work of the death and resurrection of Jesus from the nature of creation. He suggested that death and resurrection is written everywhere into creation, from crops to the stellar cycle where the death of stars manufactures the elements for a new generation of stars. He wrote,

> The principle of death and resurrection will operate anyway. . . . But its supreme example in the death and resurrection of Christ demonstrates how the process should work. . . . It is the absence of these divinely revealed in Christ qualities of love, grace and truth which makes death and resurrection so painful to bear in international, national and local and personal affairs.[59]

The image of the kernel falling into the ground means that death and resurrection is the way that Jesus must take, and that death and resurrection is the pattern for any disciple. The key question for the disciple is whether in living death and resurrection, we embody love, grace, and truth.

So, what might it mean for the church to be such a community of disciples? I am struck by this narrative, as it begins to sum up some of the themes of this lecture series.

First, the value of questions from those outside the normal theological circles of discourse. It is the arrival of the Greeks, the gentiles, that triggers the profound moment of insight. You will forgive me for drawing the parallel that as theologians we need to be open to the questions from the outside on the question of how God acts in the world, whether it be science or the rise of Pentecostalism. A God who is active in the very stuff and rhythm of creation as well as in particular events in space-time history is a God who

---

58. Barrett, *Gospel According to St John*, 352–53.
59. English, *From Wesley's Chair*, 60.

invites us to pay attention to questions that lie beyond our normal horizons of daily life.

Second, the question of how God acts in the world itself generates more questions rather than yielding an easy solution. In John 12, big questions follow this incident and teaching. For Jesus, the agony of Gethsemane is expressed in: "Now my soul is troubled, and what shall I say? 'Father, save me from this hour?' No, it was for this very reason I came to this hour. Father, glorify your name!" (John 12:28).

God's thunderous voice from heaven is heard by the crowd (vv. 28b-29), and Jesus comments that it is for their benefit even if they are unclear as to what the voice is saying (v. 30). But then John comments, "Even after Jesus had performed so many signs in their presence, they still would not believe in him"(v. 37). Signs are not an inevitable proof of the power and presence of God. They need interpretation, and both the sign and interpretation can be rejected. They do not provide easy solutions; in fact, they promote deeper reflection. As we have seen, they act often in the same way as the parables of the kingdom, giving both evidence and freedom for human beings to respond. The death and resurrection of Jesus, as church history has demonstrated, cannot be reduced to easy models of interpretation. A church focused on the death and resurrection of Jesus will maintain its epistemological humility. Miracles are not the proof of the existence and nature of God, but signs and wonders join with death on a cross to witness to a God who is active in a world of pain and joy.

Third, a community of cross and resurrection is a community who will hold together creation, redemption, and new creation as part of the sustaining and saving activity of God. The activity of God cannot be confined to the doctrine of creation, nor can such a doctrine be neglected. The cross and resurrection are an embodiment of the risky freedom that God gives to creation. It seems to me that often the church is paralyzed by fear due to the riskiness of creation. And we avoid talking about suffering and death as if it signifies failure, not only of our ministry but ultimately of God's activity. But the pattern of death and resurrection as the way to glorification shows the way that God can weave redemptive love through the pain. As T. F. Torrance stated,

> The Cross of Christ tells us unmistakably that all physical evil, not only pain, suffering, disease, corruption, death and of course cruelty and venom in animal as well as human behaviour, but also "natural" calamities, devastations, and monstrosities, are an outrage against the love of God and a contradiction of good order in

his creation. This does not allow us to regard evil and disorder in the universe as in any way intended or as given a direct function by God in the development of His creation, although it does mean that even these enormities can be made to serve His final end for the created order.[60]

The cross is about God standing with us in the mess of a fragile world, of broken people and institutions, and of unanswered questions, and at the same time it is an ultimate triumph of love over evil. The resurrection is the public vindication of this commitment and the triumph of love. It seems to me that often the church has separated Good Friday and Easter Sunday too much—into a two-leg football match where God is defeated in the first leg but puts in a better performance in the return fixture! The arc of glorification is the holding together of death and resurrection. Just as the cross is not the end of the story, neither do the marks of the cross disappear from the resurrection body of Jesus. Indeed, for some Christian traditions, these wounds are marks of glorification. For example, in Matthew Bridges "Crown Him with Many Crowns":

> Crown him the Lord of love;
> behold his hands and side,
> rich wounds, yet visible above,
> in beauty glorified.[61]

Moltmann also points out the significance of the holding together death and resurrection: "Faith in the resurrection is the faith in God of lovers and the dying, the suffering and the grieving. It is the great hope which consoles us and gives us new courage."[62]

The God who acts *is the God of death and resurrection*, and this has to be at the heart of all theological thinking. It needs to be at the heart of the mission and ministry of a church. It is the central message in the proclamation of Christian faith, foundational to the present work in caring and speaking for justice and in earthing the church's worship. Bishop Michael Perham wrote, "What will stop the descent from sparkle, that has about it a hint of heaven, to superficiality is engagement with the cross and its outworking in the lives of those who suffer. The Church's worship is never an escape from the world."[63]

---

60. Torrance, *Divine and Contingent Order*, 139.
61. Bridges, *Hymns of the Heart*.
62. Moltmann, *Coming of God*, 73.
63. Perham, *New Handbook of Pastoral Liturgy*, 8.

4.6 The Church Is a Community Open to and Amazed by the Spirit

There is an old preacher's story, overused and no doubt apocryphal. It goes back to the days when children would sit at desks with inkwells. In times well before Ricky Gervais was tormenting his RE teacher, a child was listening to a lesson on the omnipresence of God. The child raised their hand and said, "So is God in this school?" "Yes," the teacher replied. "Is God in this classroom?" "Yes," again replied to the teacher. "Is God in this inkwell?" The teacher, a victim of their own logic, had to reply "Yes." At this point the child slapped their hand over the inkwell and proclaimed, "Got him!"

The trouble with trying to define God's action in the world is perhaps summed up well in this. What is it that makes us want to explore this question? Part of it is natural curiosity about the nature of the world and the nature of God. There is something God-given in this curiosity, which means that for many of us it is simply not enough to say, "God moves in mysterious ways." But there may be a deeper motive, which is that the God of the Bible—seen in Jesus Christ and experienced in the Holy Spirit—is the one who often leaves us unsure and troubled.

The coming of the Spirit on the day of Pentecost in wind, fire, and tongues led to "bewilderment" (Acts 2:6) and people "utterly amazed" (2:7) and "amazed and perplexed" (2:12). To discover what this meant would take a different understanding of Scripture, the threat of persecution, and some painful choices of joining with the Spirit in surprising people, communities, and places. The experiences of that journey are recorded in stories, sermons, and letters in working out what the Spirit was doing. I do often wonder why the Lord did not put into the New Testament an extra book of "Frequently Asked Questions," where short and focused answers could be given to difficult questions! But the task of the theologian is to reflect not just on this material but also the work of the Spirit today. That is not an easy task, not least in the area of how God acts in the world.

In these lectures I have suggested that in acting in the world, God

- is embodied in the life, death, and resurrection of Jesus;
- is sustaining the laws of the universe;
- is transforming creation into new creation;
- is transforming the person who prays to be a collaborator in building the kingdom;

- is giving genuine but limited freedom;
- could be answering some prayers through working in the uncertainty of the quantum world and in chaotic systems;
- could work by transcending his normal ways of working for specific purposes; and
- is at work in surprising ways in the Holy Spirit.

There is no one model—either given in Scripture or in the current theological landscape—that does justice to a God who works at a multitude of levels and in so many different ways.

While John Wesley was not the first to speak about prevenient grace, it was his belief in the Spirt going ahead of us that shaped his evangelistic strategy and energy.[64] From an open communion table where the bread and wine are not restricted to those who are already members of the church but can for some be a "converting ordinance" to an openness to what we would call today charismatic signs, Wesley believed in a God who was always at work. Within the growth of early Methodism, this was not a blank check to all who claimed miraculous signs as the work of God in order to increase their own fame as leaders.[65] But it was the theological conviction of being led by the Spirit that enabled new structures of community and outreach to develop in response to God at work.

So, we return to Walter Wink's quote: "People with an attenuated sense of what is possible will bring that conviction to the Bible and diminish it by the poverty of their own experience."[66] I hope these lectures may have been just a small contribution to expand the sense of what is possible. But more than that, to echo the words of Albert Outler, believing that God is at work in the world gives Christian lifestyle its "buoyancy and gracefulness."[67] To perceive God's gracious presence and activity is to respond in worship, see this life as good, and to be freed from ultimate anxieties so that we can live intensively in the present and hopefully toward the future.

---

64. Payk, *Grace First*.
65. Rack, *Reasonable Enthusiast*.
66. Wink, "Write What You See," 6.
67. Outler, *Who Trusts in God*.

Bibliography

Abraham, William J. *Divine Agency and Divine Action*. Oxford: Oxford University Press, 2017.

———. "The Wesleyan Quadrilateral in the American Methodist-Episcopal Tradition." *Wesleyan Theological Journal* 20 (1985) 34–44.

Adams, Marilyn McCord, and Robert Merrihew Adams. *The Problem of Evil*. Oxford Readings in Philosophy. Oxford: Oxford University Press, 1990.

Agar, Jon. *Science in the Twentieth Century and Beyond*. Cambridge: Polity, 2012.

Alexander, Paul. *Signs & Wonders: Why Pentecostalism Is the World's Fastest-Growing Faith*. San Francisco: Jossey-Bass, 2009.

Allberry, Sam. *What God Has to Say About Our Bodies: How the Gospel Is Good News for Our Physical Selves*. Wheaton, IL: Crossway, 2021.

Allison, Dale C. *The Resurrection of Jesus: Apologetics, Polemics, History*. London: T&T Clark, 2021.

Amos, Jonathan. "Physics Nobel Rewards 'Spooky Science' of Entanglement." *BBC*, October 4, 2022. https://www.bbc.com/news/science-environment-63121287.

Ananthaswamy, Anil. *Through Two Doors at Once: The Elegant Experiment That Captures the Enigma of Our Quantum Reality*. London: Dutton/Penguin, 2018.

Anderson, Allan, and Walter J. Hollenweger. *Pentecostals After a Century: Global Perspectives on a Movement in Transition*. Journal of Pentecostal Theology Supplement Series. Sheffield, UK: Sheffield Academic, 1999.

Anderson, Bernhard W. *The Unfolding Drama of the Bible*. Minneapolis: Fortress, 2006.

Arbuckle, Gerald A. *The Pandemic and the People of God: Cultural Impacts and Pastoral Responses*. Maryknoll, NY: Orbis, 2021.

Ascari, Maurizio. "From Spiritualism to Syncretism: Twentieth-Century Pseudo-Science and the Quest for Wholeness." *Interdisciplinary Science Reviews* 34 (2009) 9–21.

Aspect, Alain. "Quantum Mechanics: To Be or Not to Be Local." *Nature* 446.7138 (2007) 866–67.

Aspect, Alain, et al. "Experimental Realization of Einstein-Podolsky-Rosen-Bohm Gedankenexperiment: A New Violation of Bell's Inequalities." *Physical Review Letters* 49.2 (1982) 91–94.

Astley, Jeff. *Ordinary Theology: Looking, Listening, and Learning in Theology*. Explorations in Practical, Pastoral, and Empirical Theology. Aldershot: Ashgate, 2002.

Bibliography

Astley, Jeff, et al., eds. *God in Action: A Reader*. Problems in Theology. London: T&T Clark, 2004.

Astley, Jeff, and Leslie J. Francis, eds. *Exploring Ordinary Theology: Everyday Christian Believing and the Church*. Explorations in Practical, Pastoral, and Empirical Theology. Farnham, UK: Ashgate, 2013.

Baigent, Michael, et al. *Holy Blood, Holy Grail*. New York: Delacorte, 1982.

Bailey, Mark E., et al. "Can Episodic Comet Showers Explain the 30-Myr Cyclicity in the Terrestrial Record?" *Monthly Notices of the Royal Astronomical Society* 227 (1987) 863–85.

Ballard, Paul H., and John Pritchard. *Practical Theology in Action: Christian Thinking in the Service of Church and Society*. London: SPCK, 1996.

Barbour, Ian. *When Science Meets Religion: Enemies, Strangers or Partners?* London: SPCK, 2000.

Barclay, John M. G. "The Resurrection in Contemporary New Testament Scholarship." In *Resurrection Reconsidered*, edited by Gavin D'Costa, 13–30. Oxford: Oneworld, 1996.

Barr, James. "Revelation Through History in the Old Testament and in Modern Theology." *Interpretation* 17.2 (1963) 193–205.

———. "The Theological Case Against Biblical Theology." In *Canon, Theology, and the Old Testament Interpretations: Essays in Honor of Brevard S. Childs*, edited by Gene M. Tucker et al., 3–19. Philadelphia: Fortress, 1988.

Barrett, C. K. *The Gospel According to St. John*. London: SPCK, 1978.

Barrett, Jeffrey Alan, and Peter Byrne, eds. *The Everett Interpretation of Quantum Mechanics Collected Works 1955–1980 with Commentary*. Princeton, NJ: Princeton University Press, 2012.

Barth, Karl. *The Epistle to the Romans*. Translated by Edwyn Clement Hoskyns. Oxford: Oxford University Press, 1933.

———. *The Word of God and the Word of Man*. Translated by Douglas Horton. London: Hodder and Stoughton, 1928.

Bartholomew, David J. *God of Chance*. London: SCM, 1984.

Bartlett, Robert. *The Miracles of Saint Aebba of Coldingham and Saint Margaret of Scotland*. Oxford Medieval Texts. Oxford: Clarendon, 2003.

Basinger, David. *Divine Power in Process Theism: A Philosophical Critique*. SUNY Series in Philosophy. Albany, NY: State University of New York Press, 1988.

Bassnett, Susan. "Faith, Doubt, Aid and Prayer: The Lisbon Earthquake of 1755 Revisited." *European Review* 14.3 (2006) 321–28.

Bauckham, Richard. *Gospel Women: Studies of the Named Women in the Gospels*. Grand Rapids: Eerdmans, 2002.

———. *The Theology of the Book of Revelation*. Cambridge: Cambridge University Press, 1993.

BBC. "Covid: Trump Describes His Illness 'A Blessing from God.'" BBC, October 7, 2020. https://www.bbc.com/news/world-us-canada-54455040.

Beasley Murray, George R. *John*. Word Biblical Commentary. Waco, TX: Word, 1999.

Beiser, Frederick C. *David Friedrich Strauß, Father of Unbelief: An Intellectual Biography*. Oxford: Oxford University Press, 2020.

Bell, John S. "On the Einstein Podolsky Rosen Paradox." *Physics Physique Fizika* 1.3 (1964) 195–200.

Besterman, Theodore. *Voltaire*. Oxford: Blackwell, 1976.

Bibliography

Bieler, Andrea, and Luise Schottroff. *The Eucharist: Bodies, Bread & Resurrection*. Minneapolis: Fortress, 2007.

Biernacki, Loriliai. *Panentheism Across the World's Traditions*. Oxford: Oxford University Press, 2014.

Blanco, Carlos. *Why Resurrection? An Introduction to the Belief in the Afterlife in Judaism and Christianity*. Eugene, OR: Pickwick, 2011.

Blocher, Henri. *Evil and the Cross: Christian Thought and the Problem of Evil*. Leicester, UK: Apollos, 1994.

Blumhofer, Edith Waldvogel. *Restoring the Faith: The Assemblies of God, Pentecostalism, and American Culture*. Urbana: University of Illinois Press, 1993.

Bohm, David. "A Suggested Interpretation of the Quantum Theory in Terms of 'Hidden Variables,' I." *Physical Review* 85.2 (1953) 166–79.

———. "A Suggested Interpretation of the Quantum Theory in Terms of 'Hidden Variables,' II." *Physical Review* 85.2 (1952) 180–93.

Borg, Marcus J. "The Irrelevancy of the Empty Tomb." In *Will the Real Jesus Please Stand Up: A Debate Between William Lane Craig and John Dominic Crossan*, edited by Paul Copan, 117–28. Grand Rapids: Baker, 1999.

———. "The Search Begins: The Fathers of Historical Jesus Scholarship." *Bible Review* 21.3 (2005). https://library.biblicalarchaeology.org/article/the-search-begins-the-fathers-of-historical-jesus-scholarship.

Boyd, Gregory A. *God of the Possible: A Biblical Introduction to the Open View of God*. Grand Rapids: Baker, 2000.

———. *Trinity and Process: A Critical Evaluation and Reconstruction of Hartshorne's Di-Polar Theism Towards a Trinitarian Metaphysics*. American University Studies: Series 7, Theology and Religion. New York: Lang, 1992.

Boyer, Steven D., and Christopher A. Hall. *The Mystery of God: Theology for Knowing the Unknowable*. Grand Rapids: Baker Academic, 2012.

Brannon, Michael Jeffrey. *The Hope of Life After Death: A Biblical Theology of Resurrection*. Essential Studies in Biblical Theology. Downers Grove, IL: IVP Academic, 2022.

Branton, James. "Our Present Situation in Biblical Theology." *Religion in Life* 26 (1956–1957) 5–18.

Braun, Theodore E. D., and John B. Radner. *The Lisbon Earthquake of 1755: Representations and Reactions*. Oxford: Voltaire Foundation, 2005.

Bray, Gerald. *The Personal God: Is the Classical Understanding of God Tenable?* Carlisle, UK: Paternoster, 1998.

Bridges, Matthew. *Hymns of the Heart*. 2nd ed. London: Richardson & Son, 1851.

Bristow, William. "Enlightenment." Stanford Encyclopedia of Philosophy, August 20, 2010. Revised August 29, 2017. Edited by Edward N. Zalta and Uri Nodelman. https://plato.stanford.edu/archives/fall2023/entries/enlightenment.

Brock, W. H., and R. M. Macleod. "The Scientists' Declaration: Reflexions on Science and Belief in the Wake of 'Essays and Reviews,' 1864–5." *British Journal for the History of Science* 9.1 (1976) 39–66.

Brooke, John H. *Science and Religion: Some Historical Perspectives*. Cambridge: Cambridge University Press, 1991.

Brown, Colin. *Miracles and the Critical Mind*. Exeter, UK: Paternoster, 1984.

———. *That You May Believe: Miracles and Faith Then and Now*. Grand Rapids: Eerdmans; 1985.

Bibliography

Brown, David. *Divine Humanity: Kenosis and the Construction of a Christian Theology.* Waco, TX: Baylor University Press, 2011.
Brown, Laura. *The Counterhuman Imaginary: Earthquakes, Lapdogs, and Traveling Coinage in Eighteenth-Century Literature.* Ithaca, NY: Cornell University Press, 2023.
Brown, Raymond E. *The Gospel According to John.* New York: Doubleday, 1983.
Brown, Sally A., and Patrick D. Miller. *Lament: Reclaiming Practices in Pulpit, Pew, and Public Square.* Louisville, KY: Westminster John Knox, 2005.
Browne, E. Janet. *The Power of Place.* Vol. 2 of *Charles Darwin.* London: Cape, 2002.
Browning, Don S. *Practical Theology.* San Francisco: Harper & Row, 1983.
Brunner, Emil. *The Divine-Human Encounter.* London: SCM, 1944.
———. *Revelation and Reason: The Christian Doctrine of Faith and Knowledge.* Translated by Olive Wyon. London: SCM, 1947.
Bultmann, Rudolf. *The History of the Synoptic Tradition.* Oxford: Blackwell, 1968.
———. *The New Testament and Mythology and Other Basic Writings.* Edited and translated by Schubert M. Ogden. Philadelphia: Fortress, 1984.
———. "The Question of Wonder." In *Faith and Understanding,* 242–61. Philadelphia: Fortress, 1987.
Burgess, Stanley M., and Eduard M. van der Maas, eds. *The New International Dictionary of Pentecostal and Charismatic Movements.* Grand Rapids: Zondervan, 2002.
Burns, R. M. *The Great Debate on Miracles: From Joseph Glanvill to David Hume.* Lewisburg, PA: Bucknell University Press, 1981.
Burrell, David B. "Does Process Theology Rest on a Mistake?" *Theological Studies* 43.1 (1982) 125–35.
Burreson, Kent, and Beth Hoeltke. *Death, Heaven, Resurrection, and the New Creation.* Saint Louis, MO: Concordia, 2019.
Busse, Ulrich, et al. *Miracles and Imagery in Luke and John: Festschrift Ulrich Busse.* Bibliotheca Ephemeridum Theologicarum Lovaniensium. Leuven: Peeters, 2008.
Bussey, Peter J. "Eastern Religions and Modern Physics—A Further Examination." *Science & Christian Belief* 11 (1999) 113–27.
Campbell, George. *A Dissertation on Miracles.* London: Tegg, 1824.
Capra, Fritjof. *The Tao of Physics.* London: Flamingo, 1983.
Carnley, Peter. *Resurrection in Retrospect: A Critical Examination of the Theology of N. T. Wright.* Cambridge: James Clarke, 2020.
———. *The Structure of Resurrection Belief.* Oxford: Oxford University Press, 1987.
Carson, D. A. *The Gagging of God: Christianity Confronts Pluralism.* Grand Rapids: Zondervan, 1996.
———. *The Gospel According to John.* Leicester, UK: IVP, 1991.
Cartledge, Mark J. *Practical Theology: Charismatic and Empirical Perspectives.* Studies in Pentecostal and Charismatic Issues. Carlisle, UK: Paternoster, 2003.
Case-Winters, Anna. *God's Power: Traditional Understandings and Contemporary Challenges.* Louisville, KY: Westminster John Knox, 1990.
Chase, Mitchell L. *Resurrection Hope and the Death of Death.* Short Studies in Biblical Theology. Wheaton, IL: Crossway, 2022.
Chevallier, Temple. *On the Proofs of Divine Power and Wisdom Derived from the Study of Astronomy: And on the Evidence, Doctrines, and Precepts of Revealed Religion.* Hulsean Lectures. London: J. Smith, 1827.
Childs, Brevard S. *Biblical Theology in Crisis.* Philadelphia: Westminster, 1970.

Bibliography

Chisholm, Hugh. "Paulus, Heinrich Eberhard Gottlob." *Encyclopædia Britannica*, 20:963–64. 11th ed. Cambridge: Cambridge University Press, 1911.

Cho, Anna. "Wesleyan Trinitarian Theology and Pneumatology: God's Performative Action." *HTS Teologiese Studies/Theological Studies* 78.4 (2022). doi.org/10.4102/hts.v78i4.7344.

Christianson, John Robert. *Tycho Brahe and the Measure of the Heavens*. London: Reaktion, 2020.

Clarke, Samuel. *The Evidences of Natural and Revealed Religion*. Vol. 2 of *The Works of Samuel Clarke*. London: Knapton, 1738.

Clayton, Philip. "Kenotic Trinitarian Panentheism." *Dialog* 44 (2005) 250–55.

———. "Panentheism in Metaphysical and Scientific Perspective." In *In Whom We Live and Move and Have Our Being: Panentheistic Reflections on God's Presence in a Scientific World*, edited by Philip Clayton and Arthur R. Peacocke, 73–91. Grand Rapids: Eerdmans, 2004.

———. "Panentheist Internalism: Living Within the Presence of the Trinitarian God." *Dialog* 40 (2001) 208–15.

———. *The Problem of God in Modern Thought*. Grand Rapids: Eerdmans, 2000.

Cleese, John. "The God Gene." *YouTube*, September 7, 2016. https://www.youtube.com/watch?v=wv6bB8EN2lA.

Clifton, R. K., and M. G. Regehr. "Capra on Mysticism and Modern Physics." *Science and Christian Belief* 1 (1989) 53–74.

Cobb, John B. *Grace and Responsibility: A Wesleyan Theology for Today*. Nashville: Abingdon, 1995.

Cobb, John B., and David R. Griffin. *Process Theology: An Introductory Exposition*. Philadelphia: Westminster, 1976.

Cobb, John B., and Clark H. Pinnock. *Searching for an Adequate God: A Dialogue Between Process and Free Will Theists*. Grand Rapids: Eerdmans, 2000.

Congdon, David W. "Demystifying the Program of Demythologizing: Rudolf Bultmann's Theological Hermeneutics." *Harvard Theological Review* 110.1 (2017) 1–23.

———. *The Mission of Demythologizing: Rudolf Bultmann's Dialectical Theology*. Minneapolis: Fortress, 2015.

Cook, John Granger. "Resurrection in Paganism and the Question of an Empty Tomb in 1 Corinthians 15." *New Testament Studies* 63.1 (2017) 56–75.

Cooper, Catherine Fales, and Jeremy Gregory. *Signs, Wonders, Miracles: Representations of Divine Power in the Life of the Church*. Studies in Church History. Woodbridge, UK: Boydell for the Ecclesiastical History Society, 2005.

Cooper, John W. *Panentheism, the Other God of the Philosophers: From Plato to the Present*. Nottingham, UK: Apollos, 2007.

Cotter, Wendy. *Miracles in Greco-Roman Antiquity: A Sourcebook*. London: Routledge, 1999.

Coulson, Charles A. *Science and Religion: A Changing Relationship*. Cambridge: Cambridge University Press, 1955.

Creegan, Nicola Hoggard. *Animal Suffering and the Problem of Evil*. Oxford: Oxford University Press, 2013.

Crisafulli, Virgil S., et al. *The Miracles of St. Artemios: A Collection of Miracle Stories by an Anonymous Author of Seventh Century Byzantium*. Medieval Mediterranean. Leiden: Brill, 1997.

Bibliography

Crofford, Gregory. *Streams of Mercy: Prevenient Grace in the Theology of John and Charles Wesley*. Asbury Theological Seminary Series: Study of World Christian Revitalization Movements in Pietist/Wesleyan Studies. Lexington, KY: Emeth, 2010.

Cross, Terry L. "The Rich Feast of Theology: Can Pentecostals Bring the Main Course or Only the Relish?" *Journal of Pentecostal Theology* 8.16 (2000) 27–47.

Crowe, Frederick E. "Bernard Lonergan's Thought on Ultimate Reality and Meaning." *Ultimate Reality and Meaning* 4.1 (1981) 58–89.

Crüsemann, F. "Scripture and Resurrection." In *Resurrection: Theological and Scientific Assessments*, edited by Ted Peters et al., 89–102. Grand Rapids: Eerdmans, 2002.

Crutchfield, J., et. al. "Chaos." *Scientific American* 255 (1986) 38–49.

Cullmann, Oscar. *Christ and Time*. London: SCM, 1951.

Culp, John. "Panentheism." Stanford Encyclopedia of Philosophy, December 4, 2008. Revised April 24, 2023. Edited by Edward N. Zalta and Uri Nodelman. https://plato.stanford.edu/archives/fall2023/entries/panentheism.

Curtis, Philip. *A Hawk Among Sparrows: A Biography of Austin Farrer*. London: SPCK, 1985.

Dahl, Espen. *The Problem of Job and the Problem of Evil*. Cambridge: Cambridge University Press, 2019.

Danford, John W. *David Hume and the Problem of Reason: Recovering the Human Sciences*. New Haven, CT: Yale University Press, 1990.

Darwin, Charles. *The Autobiography of Charles Darwin, 1809–1882: With Original Omissions Restored*. Edited by Nora Barlow. London: Collins, 1958.

———. "Letter to Asa Gray (Letter no. 2814)." May 22, 1860. Darwin Correspondence Project. https://www.darwinproject.ac.uk/letter/?docId=letters/DCP-LETT-2814.xml.

———. "Letter to J. D. Hooker (Letter no. 4065)." March 29, 1863. Darwin Correspondence Project. https://www.darwinproject.ac.uk/letter/?docId=letters/DCP-LETT-4065.xml.

———. *On the Origin of Species by Means of Natural Selection, or, the Preservation of Favoured Races in the Struggle for Life*. London: Murray, 1859.

Darwin, Francis, ed. *Charles Darwin: His Life Told in an Autobiographical Chapter, and in a Selected Series of His Published Letters*. London: Murray, 1902.

Davies, Brian. *The Reality of God and the Problem of Evil*. London: Continuum, 2006.

Davies, Jon. *Death, Burial and Rebirth in the Religions of Antiquity*. London: Routledge, 1999.

Davies, Paul. *The Goldilocks Enigma: Why Is the Universe Just Right for Life?* London: Allen Lane, 2006.

Davis, N. S. "Address on the Character of Dr. Edward Jenner and the History of His Discovery of the Protective Value of Vaccination." *Journal of the American Medical Association* 26.19 (1896) 915–19.

Davisson, C., and L. H. Germer. "The Scattering of Electrons by a Single Crystal of Nickel." *Nature* 119.2998 (1927) 558–60.

De Morgan, Augustus. *A Budget of Paradoxes*. London: Longmans, Green, 1872.

Dodd, C. H. *The Present Task in New Testament Studies: An Inaugural Lecture: Delivered in the Divinity School on Tuesday, 2 June*. Cambridge: Cambridge University Press, 1936.

Dodson, Jonathan K., and Brad Watson. *Raised? Finding Jesus by Doubting the Resurrection*. Grand Rapids: Zondervan, 2014.

Dodsworth, Laura. *A State of Fear: How the UK Government Weaponised Fear During the Covid-19 Pandemic*. London: Pinter & Martin, 2021.

Bibliography

Dolnick, Edward. *The Clockwork Universe: Isaac Newton, the Royal Society, and the Birth of the Modern World*. London: HarperCollins, 2011.

Dombrowski, Daniel A. *Whitehead's Religious Thought: From Mechanism to Organism, from Force to Persuasion*. Albany, NY: State University of New York Press, 2017.

Dorrien, Gary. "Modernism as a Theological Problem: The Theological Legacy of Langdon Gilkey." *American Journal of Theology & Philosophy* 28.1 (2007) 64–94.

Douglas, Kelly Brown. *Resurrection Hope: A Future Where Black Lives Matter*. Maryknoll, NY: Orbis, 2021.

Drees, Willem. *Religion, Science and Naturalism*. Cambridge: Cambridge University Press, 1996.

Dunn, James D. G. *Jesus Remembered*. Vol. 1 of *Christianity in the Making*. Grand Rapids: Eerdmans, 2003.

———. "Review: *The Resurrection of the Son of God*." *Journal of Theological Studies* 55.2 (2004) 628–32.

Earman, John. *Hume's Abject Failure: The Argument Against Miracles*. Oxford: Oxford University Press, 2000.

Eccles, John C. *How the Self Controls Its Brain*. New York: Springer, 1994.

———. "A Unitary Hypothesis of Mind-Brain Interaction in the Cerebral Cortex." *Proceedings of the Royal Society, London, Series B, Biological Science* 240.1299 (1990) 433–51.

Eddy, Paul Rhodes, and Gregory A. Boyd. *The Jesus Legend: A Case for the Historical Reliability of the Synoptic Jesus Tradition*. Grand Rapids: Baker Academic, 2007.

Ehrman, Bart D. *Jesus, Apocalyptic Prophet of the New Millennium*. Oxford: Oxford University Press, 1999.

Einstein, Albert. "Die Grundlage Der Allgemeinen Relativitätstheorie." *Annalen der Physik* 49 (1916) 769–822.

———. "On a Heuristic Viewpoint Concerning the Emission and Transformation of Light." *Annalen der Physik* 17 (1905) 132–48.

———. "Zur Elektrodynamik Bewegter Korper." *Annalen der Physik* 17 (1905) 891–921.

Einstein, Albert, et al. "Can Quantum-Mechanical Description of Physical Reality Be Considered Complete?" *Physical Review* 47.10 (1935) 777–80.

Elledge, C. D. *Resurrection of the Dead in Early Judaism, 200 BCE–CE 200*. Oxford: Oxford University Press, 2017.

English, Donald. *From Wesley's Chair*. London: Epworth, 1979.

Evans, Christopher F. *Resurrection and the New Testament*. London: SCM, 1970.

Faber, Roland. *The Becoming of God: Process Theology, Philosophy, and Multireligious Engagement*. Cascade Companions. Eugene, OR: Cascade, 2017.

Fackre, Gabriel. "Review of *Nothing Greater, Nothing Better: Theological Essays on the Love of God*, edited by Kevin J. Vanhoozer." *Theology Today* 59 (2002) 319–23.

Farrer, Austin. *Faith and Speculation*. London: A&C Black, 1967.

Fee, Gordon D. *The First Epistle to the Corinthians*. NICNT. Grand Rapids: Eerdmans, 1987.

Fiddes, Paul. "Process Theology." In *The Blackwell Encyclopedia of Modern Christian Thought*, edited by Alister McGrath, 472–76. Oxford: Blackwell, 1993.

Finney, Mark T. *Resurrection, Hell, and the Afterlife: Body and Soul in Antiquity, Judaism, and Early Christianity*. London: Routledge, 2016.

Finocchiaro, Maurice A. *The Galileo Affair: A Documentary History*. Berkeley, CA: University of California Press, 1989.

Bibliography

Finucane, Ronald C. *Miracles and Pilgrims: Popular Beliefs in Medieval England.* London: Dent, 1977.

Folse, H., and J. Faye, eds. *Niels Bohr and the Philosophy of Physics.* London: Bloomsbury, 2017.

Foster, M. B. "The Christian Doctrine of Creation and the Rise of Modern Science." *Mind* 43 (1934) 446–68.

Fowler, James W., et al. *Developing a Public Faith: New Directions in Practical Theology: Essays in Honor of James W. Fowler.* St. Louis, MO: Chalice, 2003.

Frances, Bryan. *Gratuitous Suffering and the Problem of Evil: A Comprehensive Introduction.* London: Routledge, 2013.

Frankenberry, Nancy. "Classical Theism, Panentheism, and Pantheism: On the Relation Between God Construction and Gender and Construction." *Zygon* 28 (1993) 29–46.

Fry, Edward. "Earthquakes and John Wesley." *Nature* 79.2039 (1908) 98.

Gardner, Rex F. R. "Miracles of Healing in Anglo-Celtic Northumbria as Recorded by the Venerable Bede and His Contemporaries: A Reappraisal in the Light of Twentieth Century Experience." *British Medical Journal (Clinical Research Edition)* 287.6409 (1983) 1927–33.

Garvey, Jane, et al. "Conversational Sandwiches with Tim Minchin." *Fortunately . . . with Fi and Jane* 166. Podcast aired on BBC4, November 13, 2020. https://www.bbc.co.uk/programmes/p08yd9g1.

Gaskin, J. C. A. *Hume's Philosophy of Religion.* Atlantic Highlands, NJ: Humanities, 1988.

Geivett, R. Douglas. *Evil and the Evidence for God: The Challenge of John Hick's Theodicy.* Philadelphia: Temple University Press, 1993.

George, Alison, ed. *The Quantum World: The Disturbing Theory at the Heart of Reality.* London: John Murray, 2017.

Gilkey, Langdon B. "Cosmology, Ontology and the Travail of Biblical Language." *Journal of Religion* 41 (1961) 194–205.

———. *Naming the Whirlwind: The Renewal of God-Language.* Indianapolis: Bobbs-Merrill, 1969.

Gingerich, Owen. *The Book Nobody Read: Chasing the Revolutions of Nicolaus Copernicus.* London: Arrow, 2005.

———. "Copernicus and Tycho." *Scientific American* 173.6 (1973) 86–101.

Gleick, James. *Chaos: Making a New Science.* London: Abacus, 1993.

Goodich, Michael. *Miracles and Wonders: The Development of the Concept of Miracle, 1150–1350.* Church, Faith, and Culture in the Medieval West. Aldershot, UK: Ashgate, 2007.

Goulder, Michael D. "The Baseless Fabric of a Vision." In *Resurrection Reconsidered*, edited by Gavin D'Costa, 48–61. Oxford: Oneworld, 1996.

Graham, Roderick. *The Great Infidel: A Life of David Hume.* Edinburgh: Birlinn, 2006.

Grayston, Kenneth. *The Gospel of John.* Epworth Commentaries. London: Epworth, 1990.

Grebe, Matthias, and Johannes Grössl. *T&T Clark Handbook of Suffering and the Problem of Evil.* London: T&T Clark, 2023.

Greggs, Tom. *Dogmatic Ecclesiology: The Priestly Catholicity of the Church.* Grand Rapids: Baker Academic, 2019.

———. "On the Nature, Task and Method of Theology: A Very Methodist Account." *International Journal of Systematic Theology* 20.3 (2018) 309–34.

Greig, Pete. *God on Mute: Engaging the Silence of Unanswered Prayer.* Eastbourne, UK: Kingsway, 2011.

Bibliography

Gundry, Robert H. "The Essential Physicality of Jesus' Resurrection According to the New Testament." In *Jesus of Nazareth: Lord and Christ: Essays on the Historical Jesus and New Testament Christology*, edited by Joel B. Green and Max Turner, 204–19. Grand Rapids: Eerdmans, 1994.

Gunter, W. Stephen, et al. *Wesley and the Quadrilateral: Renewing the Conversation.* Nashville: Abingdon, 1997.

Gunton, Colin. E. *Becoming amid Being: The Doctrine of God in Charles Hartshorne amid Karl Barth.* Oxford: Oxford University Press, 1978.

———. *Christ and Creation.* Carlisle, UK: Paternoster, 1992.

———. *The Promise of Trinitarian Theology.* Edinburgh: T&T Clark, 1991.

Habermas, Gary R. *Risen Indeed: A Historical Investigation into the Resurrection of Jesus.* Bellingham, WA: Lexham Academic, 2021.

Habermas, Gary R., et al. *Raised on the Third Day: Defending the Historicity of the Resurrection of Jesus.* Bellingham, WA: Lexham, 2020.

Habermas, Gary R., and Mike Licona. *The Case for the Resurrection of Jesus.* Grand Rapids: Kregel, 2004.

Hall, Christopher A., and John Sanders. *Does God Have a Future? A Debate on Divine Providence.* Grand Rapids: Baker Academic, 2003.

Hampton, Alexander J. B. *Pandemic, Ecology and Theology: Perspectives on Covid-19.* London: Routledge, 2021.

Harasta, Eva, and Brian Brock. *Evoking Lament: A Theological Discussion.* London: T&T Clark, 2009.

Hardy, Daniel. "Theology Through Philosophically Mediated Life: Donald M. MacKinnon and Nicholas Lash." In *The Modern Theologians: An Introduction to Christian Theology in the Twentieth Century*, edited by David F. Ford, 252–87. 2nd ed. Oxford: Blackwell, 1997.

Harper, Leland Royce. *Multiverse Deism: Shifting Perspectives of God and the World.* Lanham, MD: Lexington, 2020.

Harris, Steven Edward. *Refiguring Resurrection: A Biblical and Systematic Eschatology.* Waco, TX: Baylor University Press, 2023.

Harrison, Peter. "Miracles, Early Modern Science, and Rational Religion." *Church History* 75.3 (2006) 493–510.

———. "Newtonian Science, Miracles, and the Laws of Nature." *Journal of the History of Ideas* 56.4 (1995) 531–53.

———. *The Territories of Science and Religion.* Chicago: University of Chicago Press, 2015.

Hart, David Bentley. *The Beauty of the Infinite: The Aesthetics of Christian Truth.* Grand Rapids: Eerdmans, 2003.

Hartshorne, Charles. *Omnipotence and Other Theological Mistakes.* Albany, NY: State University of New York Press, 1984.

Harvey, Anthony E. "They Discussed Among Themselves What This 'Rising from the Dead' Could Mean." In *Resurrection: Essays in Honour of Leslie Houlden*, edited by Stephen Barton and Graham Stanton, 69–78 London: SPCK, 1994.

Hasker, William. *Providence, Evil, and the Openness of God.* London: Routledge, 2004.

Hasker, William, et al. *God in an Open Universe: Science, Metaphysics, and Open Theism.* Eugene, OR: Pickwick, 2011.

Hastings, W. Ross. *The Resurrection of Jesus Christ: Exploring Its Theological Significance and Ongoing Relevance.* Grand Rapids: Baker Academic, 2022.

Bibliography

Haught, John F. *Science and Religion: From Conflict to Conversation.* Mahweh, NJ: Paulist, 1995.
Hays, Richard B. *First Corinthians.* IBC. Nashville: Abingdon, 1997.
Hebblethwaite, Brian. *The Philosophical Theology of Austin Farrer.* Studies in Philosophical Theology. Leuven: Peeters, 2007.
———. *The Problem of Evil.* Farmington Papers: Ethical Issues. Oxford: Farmington Institute for Christian Studies, 1997.
Hebblethwaite, Brian, and Edward Henderson. *Divine Action: Studies Inspired by the Philosophical Theology of Austin Farrer.* Edinburgh: T&T Clark, 1990.
Heilbron, J. L. *Galileo.* Oxford: Oxford University Press, 2010.
Hein, David, and Edward Henderson. *Captured by the Crucified: The Practical Theology of Austin Farrer.* London: T&T Clark, 2004.
Heisenberg, Werner. *Physics and Philosophy.* New York: Harper & Row, 1958.
Hell, Julia, and Andreas Schönle. *Ruins of Modernity.* Politics, History, and Culture: A Series from the International Institute at the University of Michigan. Durham, NC: Duke University Press, 2010.
Helm, Paul. "Openness Theology and God's Project for the Future." *Modern Reformation* 8.6 (1999) 46–50.
———. *The Providence of God.* Downers Grove, IL: IVP, 1994.
Hengel, Martin. "The Interpretation of the Wine Miracle at Cana: John 2:1–11." In *The Glory of Christ in the New Testament Fs. G. B. Caird*, edited by L. D. Hurst and N. T. Wright, 83–112. Oxford: Clarendon, 1987.
Herrick, J. A. "Miracles and Method." *Quarterly Journal of Speech* 75.3 (1989) 321–34.
Hickey, Michael. *Rising Light: The Promise of Resurrection of the Body.* Lanham, MD: Hamilton, 2024.
Higton, Mike. *Deliver Us: Exploring the Problem of Evil.* Church Times Study Guides. Norwich, UK: Canterbury, 2007.
Hinshaw, Daniel B., and John Behr. *Thriving in the Face of Mortality: Kenosis and the Mystery of Life.* Eugene, OR: Cascade, 2023.
Holland, Peter R. *The Quantum Theory of Motion: An Account of the De Broglie-Bohm Causal Interpretation of Quantum Mechanics.* Cambridge: Cambridge University Press, 1993.
Horton, Michael Scott. *Christless Christianity: The Alternative Gospel of the American Church.* Grand Rapids: Baker, 2008.
Houghton, John T. *The Search for God: Can Science Help?* Oxford: Lion, 1995.
Houston, Joseph. *Reported Miracles: A Critique of Hume.* Cambridge: Cambridge University Press, 1994.
Hudson, Wayne. *Atheism and Deism Revalued: Heterodox Religious Identities in Britain, 1650–1800.* Burlington, VT: Ashgate, 2014.
Hume, David. *An Enquiry Concerning Human Understanding.* 1748. Edited by Tom L. Beauchamp. New York: Oxford University Press, 2000.
———. *Of Miracles.* Open Court Classics. La Salle, IL: Open Court, 1985.
Inwagen, Peter van. *The Problem of Evil: The Gifford Lectures Delivered in the University of St. Andrews in 2003.* Gifford Lectures. Oxford: Clarendon, 2006.
Iyer, Pico. "Britain: A Bolt from the Heavens." *Time*, July 23, 1984. https://time.com/archive/6698136/britain-a-bolt-from-the-heavens.
Jaki, Stanley L. *Miracles and Physics.* Front Royal, VA: Christendom, 1989.

Bibliography

Jantzen, Grace. *Becoming Divine: Towards a Feminist Philosophy of Religion*. Manchester Studies in Religion, Culture and Gender. Manchester: Manchester University Press, 1998.

———. *God's World, God's Body*. London: DLT, 1984.

Johnson, David. *Hume, Holism, and Miracles*. Cornell Studies in the Philosophy of Religion. Ithaca, NY: Cornell University Press, 1999.

Johnson, William. *Voltaire's Contribution to the Spread of Newtonianism. I, Letters from England = Les Lettres Philosophiques*. Oxford: Pergamon, 1990.

Kaku, Michio. *Physics of the Impossible: A Scientific Exploration into the World of Phasers, Force Fields, Teleportation and Time Travel*. New York: Doubleday, 2009.

Kamwendo, Z. T. "Resistance to Narratives of the Covid-19 Pandemic as an Act of God." *Zygon* 56.4 (2021) 1110–29.

Kaufman, Gordon D. "On the Meaning of 'Act of God.'" *Harvard Theological Review* 61 (1968) 175–201.

Kee, Howard Clark. *Christian Origins in Sociological Perspective: Methods and Resources*. Philadelphia: Westminster, 1980.

Keener, Craig S. *Acts*. New Cambridge Bible Commentary. Cambridge: Cambridge University Press, 2020.

———. *Miracles: The Credibility of the New Testament Accounts*. 2 vols. Grand Rapids: Baker Academic, 2011.

———. *Miracles Today: The Supernatural Work of God in the Modern World*. Grand Rapids: Baker Academic, 2021.

Kellert, Stephen H. *In the Wake of Chaos: Unpredictable Order in Dynamical Systems*. Chicago: University of Chicago Press, 1993.

Keltz, B. Kyle. *Bringing Good Even Out of Evil: Thomism and the Problem of Evil*. Lanham, MD: Lexington, 2022.

Kennedy, H. A. A. *St. Paul's Conceptions of the Last Things*. Cunningham Lectures 1904. London: Hodder and Stoughton, 1904.

Kenworthy, J. M. *The Durham University Observatory Meteorological Record*. Observatories and Climatological Research, Occasional Publication 29. Durham: Department of Geography, University of Durham, 1994.

Kenworthy, J. M., and M. D. Lowes. "The Chevalier Family: Their Contribution to Meteorology in the North-East of England." *Weather* 48.2 (1993) 51–56.

Kilby, Karen, and Rachel Davies. *Suffering and the Christian Life*. London: T&T Clark, 2020.

King, Winston L. "Some Ambiguities in Biblical Theology." *Religion in Life* 27 (1957–1958) 95–104.

Kittel, Gerhard, et al., eds. *Theological Dictionary of the New Testament*. Grand Rapids: Eerdmans, 1985.

Klein, Dietrich. *Hermann Samuel Reimarus (1694–1768): Das Theologische Werk*. Beiträge zur Historischen Theologie. Tübingen: Mohr Siebeck, 2009.

Kohlt, Franziska. "'Over by Christmas': The Impact of War-Metaphors and Other Science-Religion Narratives on Science Communication Environments During the Covid-19 Crisis." *SocArXiv*, November 10, 2020. doi:10.31235/osf.io/z5s6a.

Koopmans, Rachel. *Wonderful to Relate: Miracle Stories and Miracle Collecting in High Medieval England*. Middle Ages Series. Philadelphia: University of Pennsylvania Press 2010.

Bibliography

Korte, Anne-Marie. *Women and Miracle Stories a Multidisciplinary Exploration*. Leiden: Brill, 2004.
Langford, Thomas A., et al. *Grace Upon Grace: Essays in Honor of Thomas A. Langford*. Nashville: Abingdon, 1999.
Latourelle, René, and Matthew J. O'Connell. *The Miracles of Jesus and the Theology of Miracles*. New York: Paulist, 1988.
Laursen, John Christian, and Gianni Paganini. *Skepticism and Political Thought in the Seventeenth and Eighteenth Centuries*. UCLA Clark Library Series. Toronto: University of Toronto Press, 2015.
Leibniz, G. W. *Philosophical Papers and Letters: A Selection*. Berlin: Springer Science & Business, 2012.
Leidenhag, Joanna. "A Critique of Emergent Theologies." *Zygon* 51 (2016) 867–82.
———. *Minding Creation: Theological Panpsychism and the Doctrine of Creation*. T&T Clark Studies in Systematic Theology. London: T&T Clark, 2021.
Leidenhag, Mikael. "Is Panentheism Naturalistic: How Panentheistic Conceptions of Divine Action Imply Dualism." *Forum Philosophicum* 19 (2014) 209–25.
Lighthill, James. "The Recently Recognized Failure of Predictability in Newtonian Dynamics." *Proceedings of the Royal Society of London* A407 (1986) 35–50.
Livingstone, David. *Darwin's Forgotten Defenders*. Edinburgh: Scottish Academic, 1987.
Loftus, John W. *The Christian Delusion: Why Faith Fails*. Amherst, NY: Prometheus, 2010.
Lonergan, Bernard J. F. *Insight: A Study of Human Understanding*. Vol. 3 of *Collected Works*. Edited by Frederick E. Crowe and Robert M. Doran. Toronto: University of Toronto, 1992.
———. *Method in Theology*. London: Darton Longman and Todd, 1972.
Long, D. Stephen, and George Kalantzis. *The Sovereignty of God Debate*. Eugene, OR: Cascade, 2009.
Lorenz, Edward N. "Deterministic Non-Periodic Flow." *Journal of the Atmospheric Sciences* 20.2 (1963) 130–41.
———. "Does the Flap of a Butterfly's Wings in Brazil Set Off a Tornado in Texas?" Paper presented at the Proceedings of the 139th Meeting of the American Association for the Advancement of Science (AAAS), Cambridge, MA, December 29, 1972.
Lüdemann, Gerd. *The Acts of the Apostles: What Really Happened in the Earliest Days of the Church*. Amherst, NY: Prometheus, 2005.
Luy, David, et al. *Evil and Creation: Historical and Constructive Essays in Christian Dogmatics*. Studies in Historical and Systematic Theology. Bellingham, WA: Lexham, 2020.
MacKay, Donald M. *The Open Mind*. Leicester, UK: IVP, 1988.
———. *Science, Chance and Providence*. Oxford: Oxford University Press, 1978.
MacKinnon, Donald M. *Borderlands of Theology: And Other Essays*. Philadelphia: Lippincott, 1968.
Macnaghten, Phil. "Nanotechnology, Risk and Public Perceptions." In *In Pursuit of NanoEthics: Transatlantic Perspectives in Nanotechnology*, edited by A. M. Cutter and B. Gordijn, 167–82. Dordrecht: Springer, 2014.
MacSwain, Robert. *Solved by Sacrifice: Austin Farrer, Fideism, and the Evidence of Faith*. Studies in Philosophical Theology. Leuven: Peeters, 2013.
Maddox, Randy. "Hymn on the Lisbon Earthquake (1756)." Duke Center for Studies in the Wesleyan Tradition, September 3, 2007. https://divinity.duke.edu/sites/default/files/documents/53_Hymn_on_the_Lisbon_Earthquake_%281756%29.pdf.

Bibliography

———. "John Wesley—Practical Theologian?" *Wesleyan Theological Journal* 23 (1988) 122–47.

———. "Nurturing the New Creation: Reflections on a Wesleyan Trajectory." In *Wesleyan Perspectives on the New Creation*, edited by M. Douglas Meeks, 21–52: Nashville: Kingswood, 2004.

———. *Responsible Grace: John Wesley's Practical Theology*. Nashville: Kingswood, 1994.

———. "Responsible Grace: The Systematic Perspective of Wesleyan Theology." *Wesleyan Theological Journal* 19.2 (1984) 7–22.

———. "Seeking a Response-Able God: The Wesleyan Tradition and Process Theology?" In *Thy Nature and Thy Name Is Love: Process and Wesleyan Theologies in Dialogue*, edited by Bryan Stone and Tom Oord, 111–42. Nashville, KY: Kingswood, 2001.

Maguire, E. A., et al. "Navigation-Related Structural Change in the Hippocampi of Taxi Drivers." *Proceedings of the National Academy of Sciences USA* 97.8 (2000) 4398–403.

Manuel, Frank Edward. *The Religion of Isaac Newton*. Fremantle Lectures. Oxford: Clarendon, 1974.

Marques, José Oscar de Almeida. "The Paths of Providence. Voltaire and Rousseau on the Lisbon Earthquake." *Cadernos de História e Filosofia da Ciência. Campinas, CLE-Unicamp* 15 (2005) 33–57.

Marshall, I. Howard. *The Gospel of Luke: A Commentary on the Greek Text*. NIGTC. Exeter, UK: Paternoster, 1978.

Marxsen, Willi. *The Resurrection of Jesus of Nazareth*. Translated by Margaret Kohl. Philadelphia: Fortress, 1970.

Maudlin, Tim. *Philosophy of Physics: Quantum Theory*. Princeton Foundations of Contemporary Philosophy. Princeton, NJ: Princeton University Press, 2019.

May, Peter. "Claimed Contemporary Miracles." *Medico-Legal Journal* 71 (2003) 144–58.

———. "'Miracles Today?' A Medical Critique of Craig Keener's Miracle Claims." *Skeptic*, July 8, 2022. https://www.skeptic.org.uk/2022/07/miracles-today-a-medical-critique-of-craig-keeners-miracle-claims.

McBrayer, Justin. *The Blackwell Companion to the Problem of Evil*. Malden, MA: Wiley Blackwell, 2013.

McCready, William D. *Miracles and the Venerable Bede*. Studies and Texts (Pontifical Institute of Mediaeval Studies). Toronto: Pontifical Institute of Mediaeval Studies, 1994.

McFague, Sallie. *The Body of God: An Ecological Theology*. Minneapolis: Fortress, 1993.

———. *Models of God: Theology for an Ecological Nuclear Age*. London: SCM, 1987.

McGrew, Timothy, and Robert Larmer. "Miracles." Stanford Encyclopedia of Philosophy, October 11, 2010. Revised May 7, 2024. Edited by Edward N. Zalta and Uri Nodelman. https://plato.stanford.edu/archives/sum2024/entries/miracles.

McLeish, Tom. *Faith and Wisdom in Science*. Oxford: Oxford University Press, 2016.

———. *The Poetry and Music of Science: Comparing Creativity in Science and Art*. Oxford: Oxford University Press, 2019.

Mendes-Victor, L. A. *The 1755 Lisbon Earthquake: Revisited*. Geotechnical, Geological, and Earthquake Engineering. Dordrecht: Springer, 2009.

Miller-McLemore, Bonnie J. *The Wiley-Blackwell Companion to Practical Theology*. Wiley-Blackwell Companions to Religion. Oxford: Wiley-Blackwell, 2011.

Moltmann, Jürgen. *The Coming of God: Christian Eschatology*. London: SCM, 1996.

———. *God in Creation: An Ecological Doctrine of Creation*. San Francisco: Harper and Row, 1985.

Bibliography

———. *The Trinity and the Kingdom of God*. Translated by Margaret Kohl. London: SCM, 1981.

Moritz, Joshua M. "The Hermeneutics of Science and Scripture and Emergent Levels of Meaning." *Theology and Science* 12.1 (2014) 1–5.

Morris, Leon. *The Gospel According to John*. London: Marshall, Morgan and Scott, 1971.

Moule, C. F. D. *Miracles: Cambridge Studies in Their Philosophy and History*. London: Mowbray, 1965.

Moyers, Bill, and George Lucas. "Cinema: Of Myth and Men." *Time*, April 26, 1999.

Murphy, Nancy. "The Resurrection Body and Personal Identity: Possibilities and Limits of Eschatological Knowledge." In *Resurrection: Theological and Scientific Assessments*, edited by Ted Peters et al., 202–18. Grand Rapids: Eerdmans, 2002.

Nash, Ronald H. *Process Theology*. Grand Rapids: Baker, 1987.

NBC News. "Hurricane Katrina: Wrath of God?" *NBC News*, October 5, 2005. https://www.nbcnews.com/id/wbna9600878.

Needham, Joseph. *Science Religion and Reality*. New York: Kennikat, 1970.

Neumann, John von. *Mathematical Foundations of Quantum Mechanics*. Princeton, NJ: Princeton University Press, 1955.

Neville, Robert C. *Creativity and God: A Challenge to Process Theology*. Albany, NY: State University of New York Press, 1995.

Nimmo, Paul T., and Keith L. Johnson. *Kenosis: The Self-Emptying of Christ in Scripture and Theology*. Grand Rapids: Eerdmans, 2022.

Norton, David Fate, and Jacqueline Anne Taylor, eds. *The Cambridge Companion to Hume*. Cambridge Companions to Philosophy. 2nd ed. Cambridge: Cambridge University Press, 2009.

Ó Murchú, Diarmuid. *Quantum Theology: Spiritual Implications of the New Physics*. New York: Crossroad, 2004.

Oakley, F. "Christian Theology and the Newtonian Science: Rise of the Concepts of the Laws of Nature." *Church History* 30 (1961) 433–57.

O'Connor, Edward D. *Perspectives on Charismatic Renewal*. Notre Dame, IN: University of Notre Dame Press, 1975.

O'Donovan, Oliver. "The Political Thought of the Book of Revelation." *Tyndale Bulletin* 37 (1986) 61–94.

Oelkers, Jürgen. *Jean-Jacques Rousseau*. Continuum Library of Educational Thought. London: Continuum, 2008.

Ogden, Schubert M. "Bultmann's Project of Demythologization and the Problem of Theology and Philosophy." *Journal of Religion* 37.3 (1957) 156–73.

Oliver, Simon. "The Theodicy of Austin Farrer." *Heythrop Journal* 39 (2002) 280–97.

Oord, Thomas Jay. *Creation Made Free: Open Theology Engaging Science*. Eugene, OR: Pickwick, 2009.

———. *Defining Love: A Philosophical, Scientific, and Theological Engagement*. Grand Rapids: Brazos, 2010.

———. *The Uncontrolling Love of God: An Open and Relational Account of Providence*. Downers Grove, IL: IVP, 2015.

Orr, Brian J. *A Classical Response to Relational Theism: A Reformed Evangelical Critique of Thomas Jay Oord's Evangelical Process Theology*. Eugene, OR: Pickwick, 2022.

Orr, John. *English Deism: Its Roots and Its Fruits*. Grand Rapids: Eerdmans, 1934.

Osborn, Ronald E. *Death Before the Fall: Biblical Literalism and the Problem of Animal Suffering*. Downers Grove, IL: IVP Academic, 2014.

Bibliography

Osmer, Richard Robert. *Practical Theology: An Introduction.* Grand Rapids: Eerdmans, 2008.
Outler, Albert C. "A New Future for 'Wesley Studies': An Agenda for 'Phase III.'" In *The Future of the Methodist Theological Traditions*, edited by M. Douglas Meeks, 34–52. Nashville: Abingdon, 1985.
———. "The Wesleyan Quadrilateral in Wesley." *Wesleyan Theological Journal* 20 (1985) 7–18.
———. *Who Trusts in God: Musings on the Meaning of Providence.* New York: Oxford University Press, 1968.
Padgett, Alan. "The Roots of the Western Concept of the 'Laws of Nature': From the Greeks to Newton." *Perspectives on Science and Christian Faith* 55 (2003) 212–21.
Paice, Edward. *Wrath of God: The Great Lisbon Earthquake of 1755.* London: Quercus, 2008.
Pailin, David. *God and the Processes of Reality: Foundations of a Credible Theism.* London: Routledge, 1989.
Pannenberg, Wolfhart. *The Apostles' Creed in the Light of Today's Questions.* London: SCM, 1972.
———. *Systematic Theology.* Vol. 3. Grand Rapids: Eerdmans, 1998.
———. "Theological Appropriation of Scientific Understandings: Response to Hefner, Wicken, Eaves and Tipler." *Zygon: Journal of Religion and Science* 24 (1989) 255–71.
Parusnikova, Zuzana. *David Hume, Sceptic.* New York: Springer Berlin Heidelberg, 2016.
Patterson, Stephen J. *The God of Jesus: The Historical Jesus and the Search for Meaning.* Harrisburg: TPI, 1998.
———. "N. T. Wright, the Resurrection of the Son of God." *The Journal of Religion* 84.4 (2004) 636–37.
Paulus, Heinrich Eberh Gottlob. *Das Leben Jesu, als Grundlage einer reinen Geschichte des Urchristentums.* 2 vols. Heidelberg: Winter, 1826.
Payk, Christopher. *Grace First: Christian Mission and Prevenient Grace in John Wesley.* Tyndale Studies in Wesleyan History and Theology. Toronto: Clements Academic, 2013.
Peacocke, Arthur R. *Creation and the World of Science.* Oxford: Clarendon, 1979.
———. "Emergence, Mind, and Divine Action: The Hierarchy of the Sciences in Relation to the Human Mind–Brain–Body." In *The Re-Emergence of Emergence: The Emergentist Hypothesis from Science to Religion*, edited by Philip Clayton and Paul Davies, 256–78. Oxford: Oxford University Press, 2008.
———. *Paths from Science Towards God: The End of All Our Exploring.* Oxford: Oneworld, 2001.
———. *Theology for a Scientific Age.* London: SCM, 1990.
Peckruhn, Heike, "Rudolf Bultmann." In *Beyond the Pale: Reading Theology from the Margins*, edited by Miguel A. De La Torre and Stacey M Floyd-Thomas, 191–200. Louisville, KY: WJK, 2011.
Perham, Michael. *New Handbook of Pastoral Liturgy.* London: SPCK, 2000.
Perkins, Pheme. *Resurrection: New Testament Witness and Contemporary Reflection.* Garden City, NY: Doubleday, 1984.
Perry, John, and Joanna Leidenhag. "What Is Science-Engaged Theology?" *Modern Theology* 37.2 (2021) 245–53.
Peters, Ted. "Models of God: Deism." In *Models of God and Alternative Ultimate Realities*, edited by Jeanine Diller and Asa Kasher, 51–52. Dordrecht: Springer, 2013.

———. "Resurrection: The Conceptual Challenge." In *Resurrection: Theological and Scientific Assessments*, edited by Ted Peters et al., 297–321. Grand Rapids: Eerdmans, 2002.

———. "Theology and the Natural Science." In *The Modern Theologians*, edited by David F. Ford, 649–68. Oxford: Blackwell, 1997.

Pew Research Center. "What Lessons Do Americans See for Humanity in the Pandemic?" Pew Research Center, October 8, 2020. https://www.pewresearch.org/religion/2020/10/08/what-lessons-do-americans-see-for-humanity-in-the-pandemic.

Phillips, J. B. *Ring of Truth: A Translator's Testimony*. New York: Macmillan, 1967.

Pinnock, Clark H. *Most Moved Mover: A Theology of God's Openness*. Grand Rapids: Baker, 2001.

Pinnock, Clark H., et al. *The Openness of God: A Biblical Challenge to the Traditional Understanding of God*. Downers Grove, IL: IVP, 1994.

Pinsky, Mark I. *The Gospel According to the Simpsons: The Spiritual Life of the World's Most Animated Family*. Louisville, KY: Westminster John Knox, 2002.

Planck, Max. "Ueber das Gesetz der Energieverteilung im Normalspectrum (On the Law of Distribution of Energy in the Normal Spectrum)." *Annalen der Physik* 4.3 (1901) 553–63.

Polkinghorne, John C. "Eschatological Credibility: Emergent and Teleological Processes." In *Resurrection: Theological and Scientific Assessments*, edited by Ted Peters et al., 43–55. Grand Rapids: Eerdmans, 2002.

———. *Quantum Physics and Theology: An Unexpected Kinship*. London: SPCK, 2007.

———. *The Quantum World*. Princeton, NJ: Princeton University Press, 1984.

———. *Science and Christian Belief*. London: SPCK, 1994.

———. *Science and Providence*. London: SPCK, 1988.

———. *Theology in the Context of Science*. New Haven. CT: Yale University Press, 2009.

———. *The Work of Love: Creation as Kenosis*. Grand Rapids: Eerdmans, 2001.

Pollard, W. G. *Chance and Providence: God's Action in a World Governed by Scientific Law*. New York: Scribner's Sons, 1958.

Popper, Karl R. *Of Clouds and Clocks: An Approach to the Problem of Rationality and the Freedom of Man*. Arthur Holly Compton Memorial Lecture. St. Louis, MO: Washington University, 1966.

Porter, Stanley E. "Resurrection, the Greeks and the New Testament." In *Resurrection*, edited by Stanley E. Porter et al., 52–81. Sheffield, UK: Sheffield Academic, 1999.

Powell, Mark Allan. "Book Review: *The Resurrection of the Son of God*." *Interpretation* 58.1 (2004) 76–78.

Pupo, Spartaco. *David Hume: The Sceptical Conservative*. Politics. Riaca, Italy: Mimesis International, 2020.

Putnam, Thomas. "Hemingway on War and Its Aftermath." *Prologue* 38 (2006) 22–29.

Rack, Henry D. *Reasonable Enthusiast: John Wesley and the Rise of Methodism*. Peterborough, UK: Epworth, 2002.

Rees, Martin. *Just Six Numbers: The Deep Forces that Shape the Universe*. London: Weidenfeld and Nicholson, 2000.

Reynolds, Benjamin E., et al. *Reconsidering the Relationship Between Biblical and Systematic Theology in the New Testament: Essays by Theologians and New Testament Scholars*. Wissenschaftliche Untersuchungen Zum Neuen Testament 2 Reihe. Tübingen: Mohr Siebeck, 2014.

Bibliography

Rieder, Philip. *Miracles and Heretics: Protestants and Catholic Healing Practices in and Around Geneva 1530–1750*. Oxford: Oxford University Press, 2010.

Riley, Gregory J. *Resurrection Reconsidered: Thomas and John in Controversy*. Minneapolis: Fortress, 1995.

Riss, Richard M. "John Wesley's Reactions to the Lisbon Earthquake of 1755." PhD diss., Drew University, 2007.

Ritchie, Hannah. "There Have Been Five Mass Extinctions in Earth's History." Our World in Data, November 30, 2022. https://ourworldindata.org/mass-extinctions.

Robeck, Cecil M. *The Azusa Street Mission and Revival: The Birth of the Global Pentecostal Movement*. Nashville: Thomas Nelson, 2006.

Robinson, James M. "Jesus from Easter to Valentinus (or to the Apostles Creed)." *Journal of Biblical Literature* 101 (1982) 5–37.

Root, Andrew. *Christopraxis: A Practical Theology of the Cross*. Minneapolis: Fortress, 2014.

Rosenberg, Stanley. *Finding Ourselves After Darwin: Conversations on the Image of God, Original Sin, and the Problem of Evil*. Grand Rapids: Baker, 2018.

Rousseau, Jean-Jacques. *Letter to Beaumont, Letters Written from the Mountain, and Related Writings*. Vol. 9 of *The Collected Writings of Rousseau*. Edited by Christopher Kelly and Eve Grace. Translated by Christopher Kelly and Judith R. Bush. Hanover, NH: Dartmouth College, University Press of New England, 2001.

Rowland, Christopher. *Christian Origins: An Account of the Setting and Character of the Most Important Messianic Sect of Judaism*. London: SPCK, 1985.

Rowley, H. H. *The Unity of the Bible: W. T. Whitley Lectures Delivered at Regent's Park College, Oxford, and Rawdon College, near Leeds*. London: Carey Kingsgate, 1953.

Runyon, Theodore H. *The New Creation: John Wesley's Theology Today*. Nashville: Abingdon, 1998.

Ruether, Rosemary Radford. *Sexism and God Talk: Towards a Feminist Theology*. Boston: Beacon, 1983.

Russell, Paul, and Anders Kraal. "Hume on Religion." Stanford Encyclopedia of Philosophy, October 4, 2005. Revised November 15, 2024. Edited by Edward N. Zalta and Uri Nodelman. https://plato.stanford.edu/archives/win2024/entries/hume-religion.

Russell, Robert J. "Bodily Resurrection, Eschatology and Scientific Cosmology." In *Resurrection: Theological and Scientific Assessments*, edited by Ted Peters et al., 3–30, Grand Rapids: Eerdmans, 2002.

———. "Eschatology and Physical Cosmology: A Preliminary Reflection." In *The Far Future Universe: Eschatology from a Cosmic Perspective*, edited by George F. R. Ellis, 266–315. Radnor, PA: Templeton Foundation, 2002.

———. *Quantum Mechanics: Scientific Perspectives on Divine Action*. Vatican City State. Berkeley, CA: Vatican Observatory; Center for Theology and the Natural Sciences, 2001.

———. "Quantum Physics and the Theology of Non-Interventionist Objective Divine Action." In *The Oxford Handbook of Religion and Science*, edited by Philip Clayton, 579–95. Oxford: Oxford University Press, 2006.

Russell, Robert J., et al., eds. *Quantum Cosmology and the Laws of Nature: Scientific Perspectives on Divine Action*. Notre Dame, IN: Vatican Observatory/University of Notre Dame Press, 1993.

Russell, Robert J., et al., eds. *Chaos and Complexity: Scientific Perspectives on Divine Action*. Notre Dame, IN: Vatican Observatory/University of Notre Dame Press, 1995.

Bibliography

Russell, Robert J., et al., eds. *Neuroscience and the Person: Scientific Perspectives on Divine Action.* Notre Dame, IN: Vatican Observatory/University of Notre Dame Press, 1999.

Russell, Robert J., et al., eds. *Evolutionary and Molecular Biology: Scientific Perspectives on Divine Action.* Notre Dame, IN: Vatican Observatory/University of Notre Dame Press, 1998.

Sabourin, Leopold. *The Divine Miracles Discussed and Defended.* Rome: Catholic Book Agency, 1977.

Saler, Benson. "Supernatural as a Western Category." *Ethos* 5 (1977) 31–53.

Sanders, John. *The God Who Risks: A Theology of Providence.* Downers Grove, IL: IVP, 1998.

Schaab, Gloria. "Midwifery as a Model for Environmental Ethics: Expanding Arthur Peacocke's Models of 'Man-in-Creation.'" *Zygon* 42.2 (2007) 487–49.

Schillebeeckx, Edward. *Jesus: An Experiment in Christology.* New York: Seabury, 1979.

Schneider, John R. *Animal Suffering and the Darwinian Problem of Evil.* Cambridge: Cambridge University Press, 2021.

Schweitzer, Albert. *The Quest of the Historical Jesus: A Critical Study of Its Progress from Reimarus to Wrede.* London: Black, 1910.

Sharpe, Kevin, and Jonathan Walgate. "The Emergent Order." *Zygon* 38.2 (2003) 411–33.

Sharratt, Michael. *Galileo: Decisive Innovator.* Cambridge: Cambridge University Press, 1996.

Shaw, Jane. *Miracles in Enlightenment England.* New Haven, CT: Yale University Press, 2006.

Shelton, W. Brian. *Prevenient Grace: God's Provision for Fallen Humanity.* Wilmore, KY: Francis Asbury, 2014.

Shollenberger, George D. *God and His Coexistent Relations to the Universe: Scientific Advances of the Little Gods from Pantheism Through Deism, Theism, and Atheism to Panentheism.* Bloomington, IN: AuthorHouse, 2014.

Shrady, Nicholas. *The Last Day: Wrath, Ruin, and Reason in the Great Lisbon Earthquake of 1755.* New York: Viking, 2008.

Sider, Ronald J. "St Paul's Understanding of the Nature and Significance of the Resurrection in 1 Cor 15:1–19." *Novum Testamentum* 19 (1977) 124–41.

Simmons, Ernest L. *The Entangled Trinity: Quantum Physics and Theology.* Theology and the Sciences. Minneapolis: Fortress, 2014.

Singer, Marcus G. "The Concept of Evil." *Philosophy* 79.308 (2004) 185–214.

Sloyan, Gerard. *John.* Interpretation. Atlanta: John Knox, 1988.

Smith, James K. A., and Amos Yong, eds. *Science and the Spirit: A Pentecostal Engagement with the Sciences.* Bloomington: Indiana University Press, 2010.

Smith, Norman Kemp, and Don Garrett. *The Philosophy of David Hume: A Critical Study of Its Origins and Central Doctrines.* Houndmills, NY: Palgrave Macmillan, 2005.

Southgate, Christopher. *The Groaning of Creation: God, Evolution, and the Problem of Evil.* Louisville, KY: Westminster John Knox, 2008.

Søvik, Atle Ottesen. *The Problem of Evil and the Power of God.* Studies in Systematic Theology. Leiden: Brill, 2011.

Spencer, Nick. *Darwin & God.* London: SPCK, 2009.

Stevens, Jennifer. *The Historical Jesus and the Literary Imagination 1860–1920.* Liverpool: Liverpool University Press, 2010.

Stewart, Ian. *Does God Play Dice?* Oxford: Blackwell, 1989.

Bibliography

Stone, Bryan P., and Thomas Jay Oord. *Thy Nature and Thy Name Is Love: Wesleyan and Process Theologies in Dialogue*. Nashville, KY: Kingswood, 2001.

Strauss, David Friedrich. *The Life of Jesus Critically Examined*. Translated by George Eliot. Lives of Jesus. London: SCM, 1973.

Strelan, Rick. *Strange Acts: Studies in the Cultural World of the Acts of the Apostles*. Beihefte zur Zeitschrift für die Neutestamentliche Wissenschaft und die Kunde der Älteren Kirche. Berlin: de Gruyter, 2004.

Stump, Eleonore. *The Image of God: The Problem of Evil and the Problem of Mourning*. Oxford: Oxford University Press, 2022.

Suchocki, Marjorie Hewitt. *Trinity in Process: A Relational Theology of God*. New York: Continuum, 1997.

Surin, Kenneth. *The Turnings of Darkness and Light: Essays in Philosophical and Systematic Theology*. Cambridge: Cambridge University Press, 1989.

Swinton, John, and Harriet Mowat. *Practical Theology and Qualitative Research*. London: SCM, 2006.

Swinton, John. *Raging with Compassion: Pastoral Responses to the Problem of Evil*. Grand Rapids: Eerdmans, 2007.

Tabaczek, Mariusz. *Divine Action and Emergence: An Alternative to Panentheism*. Notre Dame, IN: University of Notre Dame Press, 2021.

Talbert, Charles H. *Reading Luke-Acts in Its Mediterranean Milieu*. Supplements to Novum Testamentum. Leiden: Brill, 2003.

Tatalović, Mićo. "Government Decisions 'Informed, Not Led by Science,' Says Vallance." *Research Professional News*, May 5, 2020. https://www.researchprofessionalnews.com/rr-news-uk-politics-parliament-2020-5-government-decisions-informed-not-led-by-science-says-vallance.

Taylor, Charles. *A Secular Age*. Cambridge: Belknap Press of Harvard University Press, 2007.

Theissen, Gerd, and Annette Merz. *The Historical Jesus: A Comprehensive Guide*. London: SCM, 1998.

Theissen, Gerd, and John Riches. *The Miracle Stories of the Early Christian Tradition*. Edinburgh: T&T Clark, 1983.

Thiselton, Anthony C. *The First Epistle to the Corinthians*. NIGTC. Grand Rapids: Eerdmans, 2000.

Thomas, Keith. *Religion and the Decline of Magic*. New York: Scribner, 1971.

Thomson, G. P., and A. Reid. "Diffraction of Cathode Rays by a Thin Film." *Nature* 119.3007 (1927) 890.

Thorson, Donald A. D. *The Wesleyan Quadrilateral: Scripture, Tradition, Reason and Experience as a Model of Evangelical Theology*. Grand Rapids: Zondervan, 1990.

Toland, John. *Christianity Not Mysterious, or, a Treatise Shewing, That There Is Nothing in the Gospel Contrary to Reason, nor Above It: And That No Christian Doctrine Can Be Properly Call'd a Mystery*. London: N.p., 1696.

———. *Tetradymus*. London: Printed and sold by J. Brotherton and W. Meadows in Cornhill, J. Roberts in Warwick-lane, W. Meres without Temple-bar, W. Chetwood in Covent-garden, S. Chapman in Pall-Mall, and J. Graves in St. James's Street, 1720.

Torrance, Thomas F. *Divine and Contingent Order*. Oxford: Oxford University Press, 1981.

———. *Space, Time and Incarnation*. London: Oxford University Press, 1969.

Trakakis, Nick, ed. *The Problem of Evil: Eight Views in Dialogue*. Oxford: Oxford University Press, 2018.

Bibliography

Truesdale, Albert. *God Reconsidered: The Promise and Peril of Process Theology.* Kansas City, MO: Beacon Hill, 2010.

Twelftree, Graham H. *Jesus the Miracle Worker: A Historical & Theological Study.* Downers Grove, IL: IVP, 1999.

Vanstone, William H. *Love's Endeavour, Love's Expense.* London: DLT, 1977.

Viney, Donald. "Process Theism." Stanford Encyclopedia of Philosophy, July 29, 2004. Revised June 4, 2022. Edited by Edward N. Zalta. https://plato.stanford.edu/archives/sum2022/entries/process-theism.

Vogel, Jeffrey. "A Self-Effacing Gardener: Divine Causality in the Theology of Austin Farrer." Christian Scholars Review, April 15, 2016. https://christianscholars.com/a-self-effacing-gardener-the-unity-of-gods-activity-in-nature-and-grace-in-the-theology-of-austin-farrer.

Voltaire. "Poem on the Lisbon Disaster." In *Toleration and Other Essays*, translated by Joseph McCabe, 255–63. New York: Putnam's Sons, 1912.

Wainwright, Geoffrey. *Doxology: The Praise of God in Worship, Doctrine and Life: A Systematic Theology.* London: Epworth, 1980.

———. *Eucharist and Eschatology.* London: Epworth, 1978.

Ward, Benedicta. *Signs and Wonders: Saints, Miracles and Prayers from the 4th Century to the 14th.* Variorum Collected Studies Series. Aldershot, UK: Variorum, 1992.

Ward, Pete. *Introducing Practical Theology: Mission, Ministry, and the Life of the Church.* Grand Rapids: Baker Academic, 2017.

Ware, James. "The Resurrection of Jesus in the Pre-Pauline Formula of 1 Cor 15.3–5." *New Testament Studies* 60 (2014) 475–98.

Warfield, Benjamin Breckinridge. *Counterfeit Miracles.* New York: Scribner's, 1918.

Warrington, Keith. *The Miracles in the Gospels: What Do They Teach Us About Jesus?* London: SPCK, 2015.

Wedderburn, A. J. M. *Beyond Resurrection.* London: SCM, 1999.

Weinberger, David. *Everyday Chaos—Technology, Complexity, and How We're Thriving in a New World of Possibility.* Boston: Harvard Business Review Press, 2019.

Wenham, David, and Craig L. Blomberg. *The Miracles of Jesus.* Vol. 6 *Gospel Perspectives.* Sheffield, UK: JSOT, 1986.

Werndl, Charlotte. "What Are the New Implications of Chaos for Unpredictability?" *British Journal for the Philosophy of Science* 60.1 (2009) 195–220.

Wesley, John. *Serious Thoughts Occasioned by the Earthquake at Lisbon: To Which Is Subjoin'd an Account of All the Late Earthquakes There, and in Other Places.* 6th ed. London: N.p., 1756.

Westerfield Tucker, Karen Beth. "'On the Occasion': Charles Wesley's Hymns on the London Earthquakes of 1750." *Methodist History* 42 (2004) 197–221.

Westfall, Richard S. *Science and Religion in Seventeenth-Century England.* Ann Arbor Paperbacks. Ann Arbor, MI: University of Michigan Press, 1973.

Weyel, Birgit, et al., eds. *International Handbook of Practical Theology.* de Gruyter Reference. Berlin: de Gruyter, 2022.

Wheeler, John A., and Wojciech H. Zurek. *Quantum Theory and Measurement.* Princeton, NJ: Princeton University Press, 1983

White, Lynn. "The Historical Roots of Our Ecological Crisis." *Science* 155 (1967) 1203–7.

White, Vernon. *The Fall of a Sparrow: A Concept of Special Divine Action.* Exeter, UK: Paternoster, 1985.

Bibliography

Whitehead, Alfred North. *Process and Reality: An Essay in Cosmology*. Gifford Lectures. Cambridge: Cambridge University Press, 1929.

Wicken, Jeffrey S. "Theology and Science in an Evolving Cosmos: A Need for Dialogue." *Zygon* 23 (1988) 45–55.

Wigelsworth, Jeffrey R. *Deism in Enlightenment England: Theology, Politics, and Newtonian Public Science*. Politics, Culture, and Society in Early Modern Britain. Manchester: Manchester University Press, 2009.

Wigner, Eugene, and Henry Margenau. "Remarks on the Mind Body Question, in Symmetries and Reflections, Scientific Essays." *American Journal of Physics* 35.12 (1967) 1169–70.

Wiles, Maurice. "Farrer's Concept of Double Agency." *Theology* 84 (1981) 243–49.

———. *God's Action in the World*. London: SCM, 1986.

Wilkinson, David. "The Accelerating Universe and New Creation: Christian Eschatology in the Face of Scientific Futility." In *Game Over? Reconsidering Eschatology*, edited by Christophe Chalamet et al., 97–110. Berlin: de Gruyter, 2017.

———. "The Activity of God: A Methodist Perspective." In *Unmasking Methodist Theology*, edited by Clive Marsh, 142–54. London: Continuum, 2004.

———. "Bible, Theology and Science: Learning from the Past and Looking to the Future." In *The Oxford Handbook of the Bible in Orthodox Christianity*, edited by E. Pentuic, 575–87. New York: Oxford University Press, 2022.

———. *Christian Eschatology and the Physical Universe*. London: T&T Clark, 2010.

———. *The Power of the Force: The Spirituality of the "Star Wars" Films*. Oxford: Lion, 2000.

———. "Proofs of the Divine Power? Temple Chevallier and the Design Argument in the 19th Century." *Scottish Journal of Theology* 68 (2015) 34–42.

———. *When I Pray, What Does God Do?* Oxford: Monarch, 2015.

———. "The Work of a Friend: Theology in the Light of the Origin of Species." *Epworth Review* 36.2 (2009) 45–65.

Wilkinson, David, and David Hutchings. *God, Stephen Hawking and the Multiverse: What Hawking Said, and Why It Matters*. London: SPCK, 2020.

Williams, Rowan. "Between the Cherubim: The Empty Tomb and the Empty Throne." In *Resurrection Reconsidered*, edited by Gavin D'Costa, 87–101, Oxford: Oneworld, 1996.

———. *On Christian Theology*. Oxford: Blackwell, 2000.

Wimber, John, and Kevin Springer. *Power Evangelism: Signs and Wonders Today*. London: Hodder and Stoughton, 1985.

Wink, Walter. "Write What You See." *Fourth R* 7 (1994) 3–9.

Witherington, Ben. "Finding Paul's Weakness." *Biblical Archaeology Review* 50.2 (2024). https://library.biblicalarchaeology.org/department/finding-pauls-weakness.

Wood, Charles M. "How Does God Act?" *International Journal of Systematic Theology* 1 (1999) 138–52.

———. *Vision and Discernment: An Orientation in Theological Study*. Scholars Press Studies in Religious and Theological Scholarship. Decatur, GA: Scholars, 1985.

Wright, Catherine. *Creation, God, and Humanity: Engaging the Mystery of Suffering Within the Sacred Cosmos*. New York: Paulist, 2017.

Wright, George E. *God Who Acts: Biblical Theology as Recital*. Studies in Biblical Theology. London: SCM, 1952.

Bibliography

Wright, N. T. *God and the Pandemic: A Christian Reflection on the Coronavirus and Its Aftermath.* Grand Rapids: Zondervan, 2020.

———. *The Resurrection of the Son of God.* London: SPCK, 2003.

Wright, Tom. "Can a Scientist Believe in the Resurrection?" James Gregory Lecture on Science, Religion and Human Flourishing, 2007. https://jamesgregory.org.uk/series-1/can-a-scientist-believe-in-the-resurrection.

Yarrow, Simon. *Saints and Their Communities: Miracle Stories in Twelfth Century England.* Oxford: Clarendon, 2006.

Yoder, Timothy S. *Hume on God: Irony, Deism and Genuine Theism.* Continuum Studies in British Philosophy. London: Continuum, 2008.

Yong, Amos. *The Spirit of Creation: Modern Science and Divine Action in the Pentecostal-Charismatic Imagination.* Pentecostal Manifestos. Grand Rapids: Eerdmans, 2011.

———, ed. *The Spirit Renews the Face of the Earth: Pentecostal Forays in Science and Theology of Creation.* Eugene, OR: Pickwick, 2009.

Young, Thomas. "The Bakerian Lecture: Experiments and Calculation Relative to Physical Optics." *Philosophical Transactions of the Royal Society of London* 94 (1804) 1–16.

Zilsel, Edgar. "The Genesis of the Concept of Physical Law." *Physics Review* 51 (1942) 245–79.

Zukav, Gary. *The Dancing Wu Li Masters: An Overview of the New Physics.* London: Rider, 1990.

Zwiebach, Barton. *Mastering Quantum Mechanics: Essentials, Theory, and Applications.* Cambridge: MIT, 2022.

General Index

A State of Fear, 92
Abraham, W.J., 32, 44
accelerating universe, 35
Adams, M.M., 23
Adams, R.M., 23
Agar, J., 8
Alexander, P., 66
Allberry, S., 75
Allison, D.C., 75
analogy, 57
Ananthaswamy, A., 10
Anderson, A., 66
Anderson, B.W., 22
anthropic balances, 82
antisemitism, 24
anti-supernaturalism, 53
apologetics, 2, 20, 23, 28, 55–56, 71 72, 92
Aquinas, Thomas, 3, 55
Arbuckle, G.A., 86
argument from design, 2, 6–7, 28–29, 42, 79, 80, 82–83
Aristotle, 3–4
Arminianism, 37
Ascari, M., 16
ascension, 62, 71, 74
Aspect, A., 1, 16
Astley, J., 51
Augustine, 7
awe, 67, 82
Azusa Street, 66

Baigent, M., 61
Bailey, M.E., 24
Ballard, P.H., 98
Banks, Joseph, 93
Barbour, I., 32, 98
Barclay, J.M.G., 73
Barr, J., 22, 23
Barrett, C.K., 67–68, 101–2
Barrett, J.A., 10
Barth, K., 21
Bartholomew, D., 50
Bartlett, R., 66
Basinger, D., 32
Bassnett, S., 85
Bauckham, R., 23, 46, 71
Beasley Murray, G.R., 67
beauty, 29, 30, 104
Behr, J., 36
Beiser, F.C., 62
Bell, J.S., 16
Benedict XVI, 54
Besterman, T., 57
biblical theology, 21–23, 42, 56
Bieler, A., 75
Biernacki, L., 33
Big Bang, 35
Blanco, C., 73
Blocher, H., 24
Blomberg, C., 67
Blumhofer, E.W., 66
bodily resurrection, 23, 30, 46, 48, 56, 61–62, 68, 70–76, 78, 85, 101–5

General Index

Bohm, D., 11
Bohr, Neils, 10
Borderlands of Theology and Other Essays, 98
Borg, M.J., 62, 73
bottom-up approach, 97
Boyd, G.A., 32, 48, 53
Boyer, S.D., 89
Boyle, Charles, 5
Boyle, Robert, 6, 56, 59
Brahe, Tycho, 3–4
brain, 10, 17, 34, 94
Brannon, M.J., 74
Branton, J., 22
Braun, T.E.D., 84
Bray, G., 36
Bridges, Matthew, 104
Bristow, W., 28
Brock, B., 88
Brock, W.H., 97
Brooke, J.H., 5, 97
Brown, C., 54
Brown, D., 36
Brown, L., 84
Brown, R., 67
Brown, S.A., 88
Browne, E.J., 79
Browning, D.S., 98
Brunner, E., 22
Buddhism, 16
Bultmann, R., 25–27, 43, 53, 71
Burgess, S.M., 66
burning bush, 22
Burns, R.M., 7, 56, 62
Burrell, D.B., 32
Burreson, K., 75
Busse, U., 67
Bussey, P.J., 16
Byrne, P., 10

Caccini, Tommaso, 4
Cage, Nicholas, 15
Calvin, John, 45, 66
Calvinism, 37, 45
Campbell, G., 60
Capra, F., 16–17
Carnley, P., 70–71

Carson, D.A., 36, 67, 101
Cartledge, M.J., 98
Case-Winters, A., 32
causal joint, 41
chance, 12, 36, 45, 50
chaos, 3, 8, 11–13, 15, 17, 18, 19, 25, 39, 40, 41, 43–44, 57, 63–65, 98, 100, 106
Chase, M.L., 74
Chevallier, Temple, 80–83
Childs, B.S., 22
Chisholm, H., 61
Cho, A., 48
Christianson, J.R., 4
Christology, 48, 99
Clarke, Samuel, 7, 56, 59
classical theism, 31, 33, 37
Clauser, John, 1
Clayton, P., 31, 33–34, 36
Cleese, John, 15
Clifton, R.K., 16
climate emergency, 2
clockwork universe, 3, 6–8, 12–13, 17–19, 27–30, 33–35, 44, 60, 96
Cobb, J.B., 31, 36, 49
Collins, A., 5
conflict model, 7, 91
Congdon, D.W., 26
conversion, 1, 49
Cook, J.G., 73
Cooper, C.F., 66
Cooper, J.W., 6, 34
Copenhagen interpretation of quantum theory, 10
Copernicus, Nicolaus, 4
Corbridge, Stuart, 90
Cotter, W., 67
Coulson, C.A., 82
covenant, 38
Covid virus, 91, 93, 95
creatio ex nihilo, 38, 46, 59, 75
creatio ex vetere, 75
creation, 20, 25, 28–30, 32, 36, 45–49, 67, 73–76, 79, 83, 85, 87–88, 92–93, 95, 102–5
Creegan, N.H., 24
Crisafulli, V.S., 66

130

General Index

critical realism, 14, 18, 39
Crofford, G., 49
cross, 48, 61, 72, 76, 78, 99, 101, 103–4
Cross, T.L., 37
Crowe, F.E., 14
Crown Him with Many Crowns, 104
Crüsemann, F., 72
Crutchfield, J., 12
Cullmann, O., 22
Culp, J., 33
Curtis, P., 41

Dahl, E., 24
Danford, J.W., 55
Darwin, Annie, 80, 81
Darwin, Charles, 24, 79–81, 83
Darwin, Emma, 80
Darwin, F., 80
Davies, B., 23, 24, 82
Davies, J., 71
Davies, P., 82
Davies, R., 24
Davis, N.S., 93
Davisson, C., 9
Day, David, 68
de Broglie, Louis, 11
De Morgan, A., 6
death and resurrection of Jesus, 25, 48, 61, 74, 99, 102–5
Death Star, 20
death, 79–81, 83, 87
deism, 5–7, 27–30, 34, 61, 99
demiurge, 29
demythologization, 26, 96
Dionysus, 68
divine action, 2, 21, 26, 65, 67, 70, 75, 77, 87
Docetism, 71
Dodd, C.H., 22
Dodson, J.K, 75
Dodsworth, L., 92
Dolnick, E., 6
Dombrowski, D.A., 31
Dorrien, G., 22
double agency, 41–42
Douglas, K.D., 75
dualism, 22, 34, 74

Dunn, J.D.G., 23, 67, 70
Durham University, 81, 90

Earman, J., 54, 62
earthquakes, 41, 79, 83–85, 87, 91
Eccles, J.C., 17
ECLAS, 86–87, 91, 100
ecochurch, 95
ecological crisis, 93
Eddy, P.R., 53
Ehrman, B.D., 61
Einstein, Albert, 2, 8–9, 15–16, 64
electromagnetism, 8–9, 63
Elledge, C.D., 73
embodiment, 34
emergence, 15, 33, 36
empirical science, 3–4, 14, 24
empty tomb, 71–75
end of the universe, 2, 38, 46–47, 75
English, D., 44, 102
Enlightenment, 6, 28, 66
epistemological problem of quantum theory, 11
EPR paradox, 15
eschatology, 36, 46–47, 49, 67, 73, 88
eternal, 31, 62, 102
Eucharist, 75, 88, 106
Evangelical Theological Society, 37
evangelism, 106
Evans, C.F., 71
Everett, Hugh, 10
evolution, 24, 30, 33, 36 79–80, 83
eyewitness accounts, 60, 65

Faber, R., 31
Fackre, G., 38
Farrer, A., 41, 42
Faye, J., 10
fear, 92, 95, 103
Fee, G.D., 73
feeding of the five thousand, 61
feminist theology, 34, 96
Fetter, Ellen, 11
Fiddes, P., 32
Finney, M.T., 73
Finocchiaro, M.A., 4
Finucane, R.C., 66

General Index

Flanders, Ned, 51
Folse H., 10
Fortunately . . . with Fi and Jane, 86
Foster, M.B., 57
Fowler, J.W., 98
Frances, B, 23
Francis, L., 51
Frankenberry, N., 34
free- process defense, 39
freedom, 17–18, 20, 29, 30, 32, 35–39, 42, 43, 45–50, 54, 65, 103, 106
freewill, 17, 38–39
Fry, E., 85

Galapagos Islands, 79
Galileo, 3, 4
Gardner, R.F.R., 66
Garrett, D., 55
Garvey, Jane, 86
Gaskin, J.C.A., 56
Geivett, R.D., 23
general resurrection, 74
generalized empirical method, 14
George A., 8
Germer, L.H., 9
Gervais, Ricky, 21, 42, 105
Gethsemane, 103
Gilkey, L.B., 22, 96
Gingerich, O., 4
Gleick, J., 12
global church, 52, 65, 77
Glover, Fi, 86
God as creator, 19, 32, 46–47, 49, 57, 65, 75, 79, 89, 93, 95
God as sustainer, 2, 29–30, 33–34, 40, 46, 48, 57, 59, 65, 70, 87, 93–94, 103, 105
god of the gaps, 40, 44–45, 65, 82
God's agency, 11, 20, 30
Goodich, M., 66
Goulder, M., 71
grace, 38, 48–50, 90, 102, 106
Graham, R., 55
gravity, 8
Gray, Asa, 80
Grayston, K., 69
Grebe, M., 23

Greggs, T., 48
Gregory, J., 66
Greig, P., 52
Griffin, D.R., 31
Grössl, J., 23
Gundry, R.H., 72
Gunter, W.S., 44
Gunton, C., 32, 47, 48

Habermas, G.R., 75
Hall, C.A., 36, 89
Hamilton, Margaret, 11
Hampton, A.J.B., 86
Harasta, E., 88
Hardy, D., 98
Harper, L.R., 28
Harris, S.E., 74
Harrison, P., 6–7, 55–56, 59–60, 62–63
Hart, D.B., 26
Hartshorne, C., 30–31, 35
Harvey, A.E., 71
Hasker, W., 36, 39
Hastings, W.R., 75
Haught, J.F., 98
Hawking, Stephen, 18, 35
Hays, R.B., 73
healing, 65–67, 78, 80
Hebblethwaite, B., 23, 41
Heilbron, J.L., 4
Hein, D., 41
Heisenberg, W., 9–10
Hell, J., 84
Helm, P., 36, 49–50
Henderson, E., 41
Hengel, M., 69
hermeneutics, 96
Herrick, J.A., 61
Hick, John, 23, 24
Hickey, M., 75
hiddenness of God, 26, 40, 42, 65
Higton, M., 24
Hinduism, 16
Hinshaw, D.B., 36
HMS Beagle, 79
Hoeltke, B., 75
holiness, 49, 90
Hollenweger, W.J., 66

General Index

Holocaust, 24, 25
Holy Spirit, 32, 48–49, 66, 87, 99, 100, 105–6
Hooker, Jospeh, 79
hope, 46, 75, 86, 92, 95
Horton, M.S., 29
Houghton, J.T., 42
Houston, J., 54
Hudson, W., 28
human agency, 2, 20, 48, 87–88, 94
Hume, David, 28, 52, 54, 55–57, 59–60, 62–63
Hutchings, D., 35
Hymns Occasioned by the Earthquake, March 8, 1750, 84
hymns, 84, 85

Ichneumonidae wasp, 80
immanence, 6, 14, 26, 33–34, 36, 43, 46–48
immutability, 31, 37
incarnation, 30, 36, 48, 85, 101
information theory, 94
injustice, 21, 24, 94, 104
intelligibility, 14
intercession, 88
intervention, 5, 10, 28, 44, 47, 62, 87
Inwagen, P., 23
Iyer, P., 85

Jaki, S.L., 54
Jantzen, G., 34
Jenkins, David, 85, 95
Jenner, Edward, 93, 94
Jesus, 3, 21, 23, 25–27, 30, 36, 42, 48, 52–53, 61–62, 66, 67, 68–78, 83, 87, 89, 92, 95, 99, 101–105
Job, 24, 45
Johnson, Boris, 91
Johnson, D., 54
Johnson, K.L., 36
Johnson, W., 57
judgment, 62, 84, 85
justice, 104

Kaku, M., 64
Kalantzis, G., 36

Kamwendo, Z.T., 87, 92
Kant, Immanuel, 14, 84
Kaufman, G.D., 43
Kee, H.C., 53
Keener, C.S., 53, 57, 65, 67
Kellert, S.H., 12
Keltz, B.K., 24
Kennedy, H.A.A., 74–75
kenosis, 35–36, 39
Kenworthy, J.M., 81
Kilby, K., 24
King, W.L., 22
kingdom, 61, 66–67, 103, 105
Kittel, G., 63
Klein, D., 61
Kohlt, F., 91
Koopmans, R., 66
Korte, A-M., 66
Kraal, A., 55
Krause, Karl, 33

lament, 88, 89
Langford, T.A., 49
Laplace, Pierre-Simon, 5
Larmer, R., 54
Latourelle, R., 67
Laursen, J.C., 55
laws of nature, 4, 6–8, 12–13, 17, 26, 29–30, 32–34, 40–43, 45, 54, 57, 59–65, 76, 80, 82, 87, 94, 96, 105
Lazarus, 72
Leap of Faith, 78
led by the science, 95–96
Leibniz, G.W., 5
Leidenhag, J., 24, 34–35
Leidenhag, M., 31, 34
liberation theology, 96
Licona, M., 75
Lighthill, J., 13
Lisbon earthquake, 83–85, 91
liturgy, 85
Livingstone, D., 83
lockdown, 95
Locke, John, 28, 56
Loftus, J.W., 23
London taxi drivers, 34
Lonergan, B., 14–15

General Index

Long, D.S., 36
Lorenz, E.N., 11–12
Lowes, M.D., 81
Lucas, George, 19–20
Lüdemann, G., 53–54
Luy, D., 24

MacKay, D.M., 42, 94, 95
MacKinnon, D.M., 98
Macleod, R.M., 97
Macnaghten, P., 95
MacSwain, R., 41
Maddox, R., 43–46, 49, 85
Maguire, E.A., 34
Manuel, F.E., 60
many-worlds interpretation of quantum theory, 10
Margenau, H., 10
Marques, J.O., 84
Marshall, I.H., 72
Martin, Steve, 78
Marxsen, W., 73
mass extinctions, 24
Maudlin, T., 8
Maxwell, James Clerk, 8–9, 63
May, P., 54, 65–66
McBrayer, J., 23
McCready, W.D., 66
McFague, S., 34
McGrew, T., 54
McLeish, T., 98
measurement problem in quantum theory, 10
Mendes-Victor, L.A., 84
Merz, A., 62
meteorology, 7, 11–12, 40
Miller, P.D., 88
Miller-McLemore, B.J., 98
Minchin, Tim, 78, 86
ministry, 2–3, 6, 20, 29, 43, 66, 76–78, 87, 90, 100, 103–4
miracle, 3, 6–7, 22, 26–30, 38, 51–57, 59–70, 76–78, 80, 88, 96
mission, 2–3, 6, 23, 26, 29, 66, 76–77, 87, 100, 104
Moltmann, J., 35–36, 47, 104
Moritz, J.M., 96
Morris, L., 67
Moses, 22
Mowat, H., 98
Moyers, B., 20
Murphy, N., 76
mystery, 14, 20–21, 27, 42, 45, 72, 89, 94
myth, 23, 26, 62, 70, 88, 95

Napoleon, 5
Nash, R.H., 31
natural disasters, 85, 87
natural theology, 14, 48, 99
Natural Theology, 6, 79, 80
Needham, J., 57
Nelmes, Sarah, 93
Neumann, J., 10
Neville, R.C., 32
new atheism, 7
new creation, 38, 45–48, 73–75, 85, 88, 103, 105
Newton, Isaac, 1, 3, 4–9, 12–13, 16, 18, 30, 59, 60, 62, 64, 96
Newtonian worldview, 2–3, 6, 8, 12–13, 26–27, 30–34, 40, 43, 53–54, 57, 59, 60, 63–64, 77, 96
Nimmo, P.T., 36
Norton, D.F., 55

Ó Murchú, D., 11
O'Connell, M.J., 67
O'Connor, E.D., 66
O'Donovan, O., 74
Oakley, F., 57
Oelkers, J., 60
Ogden, S.M., 26
Oliver, S., 42
omnipotence, 23–24, 31, 37, 59–60, 80
omniscience, 37–38
On the Origin of Species, 79
On the Proofs of Divine Power and Wisdom Derived from the Study of Astronomy, 81
On the Revolutions of the Celestial Spheres, 4
Oord, T.J., 35–37, 39
openness theology, 17–18, 21, 35–40, 47–48, 50, 64, 95, 106

General Index

orbit of Mercury, 8, 64
order, 29, 32–33, 35–36, 45, 47, 59, 69, 79, 90–91, 94, 98, 103–4, 106
ordinary theology, 51
Orr, B.J., 32
Orr, J., 28
orrery, 5
Osborn, R.E., 24
Osiander, Andreas, 4
Osmer, R.R., 98
Outler, A.C., 44, 45, 50, 106

Padgett, A., 57
pagan view of nature, 94
Paganini, G., 55
Paice, E., 84
Pailin, D., 31
Paley, William, 6, 79, 81
pandemic, 2, 19, 86–87, 90–92, 95
Pandora's box, 95
panentheism, 6, 33–36
Pannenberg, W., 7–8, 49, 73
pantheism, 6, 33–34, 59
parousia, 74
Parusnikova, Z., 55
pastoral care, 20
Patterson, S.J., 70, 73
Paulus, H.E.G., 61–62
Payk, C., 106
Peacocke, A.R., 15, 33
Peckruhn, H., 26
Pentecostalism, 37, 66, 99, 102
Perham, M., 104
Perkins, P., 71
Perry, J., 24
persuasion, 31
Peters, T., 28, 73, 98
Phillips, J.B., 70
Phipps, James, 93
photoelectric effect, 9
pillar of cloud and fire, 61
Pinnock, C.H., 36–38, 47
Pinsky, M.I., 52
Piper, Don, 78
Planck, M., 9
pneumatology, 48, 99
Podolsky, B., 15, 16

Polkinghorne, J.C., 8, 11, 13–14, 16–18, 24, 39, 40–42, 63, 65, 73, 75, 96–97
Pollard, W.G., 17
Popper, K.R., 13
Porter, S.E., 71
Powell, M.A, 70
practical theology, 98
prayer, 2, 27, 37–38, 52, 77, 80, 85, 88–90
preaching, 52, 73, 85–86, 88
predictability, 13, 17, 19, 44
Principia, 5, 13
Pritchard, J., 98
problem of evil, 2, 7, 20–25, 29–32, 34–35, 38–39, 41–43, 45, 47–48, 50, 54, 77–80, 85, 87–88, 91, 103–4
process theology, 30–33, 36–38
prologue of John, 67
proof of the existence of God, 28, 82
providence, 3, 17–18, 20–21, 25, 29, 36–37, 41–51, 76, 84, 96, 99, 100
provisionality, 14, 18, 45, 57, 63, 65, 95–96
Ptolemy, 3
public health, 92
Pupo, S., 55
Putnam, T., 91

quantum computing, 2, 16
quantum entanglement, 1–3, 16
quantum mechanics, 1
quantum theory, 1, 3, 8–11, 13–19, 39–40, 43–45, 57, 63–64, 98, 100, 106
quest for the historical Jesus, 61

Rack, H.D., 106
radiation from a heated body, 8
Radner, J.B., 84
reason, 28–29, 44–45, 79, 82–83, 85, 87, 89, 93, 103
redemption, 46, 49, 74–75, 85, 103
reductionism, 15
Rees, M., 82
Reformation, 55, 66
Regehr, M.G., 16
Reid, A., 9

General Index

Reimarus, Hermann Samuel, 61–62
relativity, 1, 8, 64
reliability of witnesses, 52
religious experience, 2, 29, 71
resuscitation, 65, 72
revelation, 21–22, 42, 72, 81–83, 89
Reynolds, B.E., 22
Riches, J., 67
Rieder, P., 66
Riley, G.J., 71
Riss, R.M., 85
Ritchie, H., 24
road to Emmaus, 72
Robeck, C.M., 66
Robinson, J.M., 71
Roosevelt, Franklin D., 92
Root, A., 98
Rosen, N., 15
Rousseau, Jean-Jacques, 60, 84
Rowland, C., 67
Rowley, H.H., 22
Runyon, T.H, 45
Russell, P., 55
Russell, R.J., 11, 17, 24, 25, 55, 73, 76

Sabourin, L., 53
Saler, B., 53
salvation history, 22
Sanders, J., 36, 37
Satan, 45
Schaab, G., 34
Schillebeeckx, E., 71
Schneider, J.R., 24
Schönle, A., 84
Schottroff, L., 75
Schweitzer, A., 61
science as a gift, 82, 97
science as Christian vocation, 20
Science for Seminaries, 100
science-engaged theology, 24–25
Scientists in Congregations, 100
seismology, 84
self-limitation of God, 29. 36
Serious Thoughts Occasioned by the Late Earthquake at Lisbon, 84
Sharpe, K., 15
Sharratt. M., 4

Shaw, J., 66
Shelton, W.B., 49
Shepherd, Linda Evans, 78
Sherlock, Thomas, 56
Shollenberger, G.D., 28
Shrady, N., 84
Sider, R.J., 73
signs and wonders, 23, 40, 63, 66–70, 77–78, 90, 94–95, 99, 103, 106
Simmons, E.L., 11
simplicity, 37, 96
sin, 49
Singer, M.G., 24
Sloyan, G., 67
smallpox, 93
Smith, J.K.A., 100
Smith, N.K., 55
Southgate, C., 24
sovereignty of God, 2, 37, 38, 46, 50, 74
Søvik, A.O., 23
speed of light, 64
Spencer, N., 80
Spinoza, Baruch, 59
spooky action at a distance, 2, 15
Springer, K., 66
Star Wars, 19, 20
Stevens, J., 61
Stewart, I., 40
Stone, B.P., 37
Strauss, David Friedrich, 62
Strelan, R., 67
Stump, E., 24
Suchocki, M.H., 32
suffering, 21, 23–24, 29, 36, 38, 52, 79, 85, 87, 89, 93, 103–4
Sunak, Rishi, 19–20
Sunday Bloody Sunday, 88
Surin, K., 24
Swinton, J., 24, 98
swoon theory, 61

Tabaczek, M., 34
Talbert, C.H., 54
Tatalović, M., 96
Taylor, C.A., 27, 29
Taylor, J.A., 55
The Bridgewater Treatises, 6

General Index

The Declaration of Students of the Natural and Physical Sciences, 97
The Phantom Menace, 20
The Simpsons, 51
Theissen, G., 62, 67
theological formation, 90
theological method, 43–44
Thiselton, A.C., 73
Thomas, K., 66
Thomson, G.P., 9
thorn in the flesh, 90
Thorson, D.A., 44
Tindal, Matthew, 28
Toland, John, 61
top-down causation, 34
Torrance, T.F., 64, 103, 104
training of church leadership, 100
Trakakis, N., 23
transcendence, 26–27, 29, 33–34, 36, 38, 43, 46–48, 95
transformation, 46, 69, 72–75
trauma, 91
Trinity, 11, 32–34, 36, 47–49, 99
triumph of God, 20, 35, 38–39, 43, 47–48, 50, 68, 91, 94, 104
Truesdale, A., 32
Trump, Donald, 91
Twelftree, G.H., 62

Uncertainty Principle, 9
universal law of gravitation, 4
universality of laws, 8, 29–30
universe as God's body, 33, 34, 46
unpredictability, 7, 12, 18, 19, 39, 44, 79

vaccination, 91–94
vale of soul making, 23
Vallance, Patrick, 96
van der Maas, E.M., 66
Vanstone, W.H., 35
verisimilitude, 18, 57
Viney, D., 31, 32
violations of natural law, 57
Vogel, J., 41
Voltaire, 57, 84
vulnerability, 34–36
Wainwright, G., 48, 88

Walgate, J., 15
walking on the water, 61
war, 91
Ward, B., 66
Ward, P., 98
Ware, J., 73
Warfield, B.B., 66
Warrington, K., 67
Watson, B., 75
Wedderburn, A.J.M., 71
wedding in Cana, 67, 68
Weinberger, D., 12
Wenham, D., 67
Werndl, C., 12
Wesley, Charles, 84–85
Wesley, John, 37, 43–45, 48–49, 84–85, 102, 106
Wesleyan quadrilateral, 44
Wesleyan theology, 31, 36, 42–45, 47–50
Westerfield Tucker, K.B., 85
Westfall, R., 7
Weyel, B., 98
Wheeler, J.A., 10
Whiston, William, 5
White, Lynn, 92–93
White, V., 30
Whitehead, Alfred North, 30, 31
Wicken, J.S., 49
Wigelsworth, J.R., 6, 28
Wigner, E., 10
Wilde, Oscar, 61
Wiles, M., 29–30, 32, 42–43, 47–48, 70
Wilkinson, D., 20–21, 35, 38, 46, 72–73, 80, 83, 96
Williams, R., 71
Wimber, J., 66, 77
Wink, Walter, 3, 42–43, 53, 106
Witherington, B., 90
women as first witnesses of the resurrection, 71
Wood, C.M., 44, 47–48, 99
worship, 68, 78, 85–86, 88–89, 104, 106
Wright, C., 23
Wright, G., 21
Wright, N.T., 23, 70, 73, 86

General Index

Yarrow, S., 66
Yoder, T.S., 28
Yong, A., 100
Young, T., 9

Zeilinger, A., 1
Zilsel, E., 57
Zukav, G., 16, 17
Zurek, W.H., 10
Zwiebach, B., 8

Scripture Index

Psalm
13:1–2   88
19   81

Eccl
9:11–12   45

Isa
45:7   45
65:17–25   46

Dan
12:2–3   71

Matt
5:45   92
9:38   27
10:5   27
13:3–9   102
13:24–31   102
28:17   72

Mark
4:3–9   102
4:26–29   102
4:30–32   102
16:1–8   72

Luke
8:4–8   102
13:18   102
15:1–10   38
15:11–32   38
24:13–35   72
24:37   72

John
2:1–11   67
12   101, 103
20:14   72
20:19–20   72
21:4, 12   72

Acts
2:6–12   105

Romans
8   85

1 Corinthians
13   92
15:20–28   73
15:22   74
15:45   74

2 Corinthians
12:7b–10   90

www.ingramcontent.com/pod-product-compliance
Lightning Source LLC
Chambersburg PA
CBHW031501160426
43195CB00010BB/1062